OWNING YOURSELF

Learn how to create an income that
continues long after your work is done

Paula Pritchard

Printed in the United States of America
For information about additional materials visit:
www.mlmmadesimple.com

Acknowledgements

My success in network marketing and ultimately the writing of this book is a direct result of the encouragement I have received over the years from some very special people.

First of all, I'd like to thank my brothers, Bill and Roger. Their example of hard work and discipline has always set the standard for me to never settle for mediocrity in my own performance. I don't think they even realized I was watching.

To Jody Victor, my first and only mentor, I owe him so much. He inspired and taught me the difference between good and evil and for that I am grateful. He said we are all responsible for our own success and with that I realize comes responsibility. I am a better leader because of Jody.

To Harold Miller, I want to thank him for being the loving, caring example of what this business can be. He deserves all the happiness in the world.

To Kathy Robbins, who is the most morally sound, honest and caring person I know. She has been a wonderful friend and confidant through thick and thin. Her constant encouragement over the years has brought this book to fruition.

And lastly, I thank Tom Murphy whose constant prodding and support made this book become a reality.

Table of Contents

Preface to the Second Edition

I hesitated to write a second edition to this book. The book has helped thousands of network marketers around the world understand the basic principles of building a business. The changes in technology over the last few years however, have made an enormous impact on the way we do business. I felt it important to include the ways technology can both help and hurt your business.

You will find that the fundamental principals of network marketing do not change. The business is still relationship driven and where technology has caused relationship building to take a back seat, the business has suffered. The new technology and the Internet can be used to enhance relationships and communication. The best business will always be one that combines high tech and high touch.

My goal in the second edition remains the same as it was in the original: to provide you with the information that will help you build the kind of business that provides an ongoing income that continues long after your work is finished.

Paula Pritchard

Preface to the First Edition

Early in life it became clear to me that freedom is a relative term. The loss of freedom seems clear when referring to an oppressed country run by a dictator or a convict in a penal institution. However, even though law-abiding US citizens are promised certain freedoms by the Constitution, some people argue that those freedoms are in actuality based on gender, education and race. In my opinion, there has never been a more obvious determinant of freedom than financial status.

After all, we are a free people living in a free country, but until we are financially free, someone dictates where we will work, where we live, the quality of schools to which we send our children, the size of our home, the length of our vacations and the kind of car we drive. In actuality, until we're financially free, we're not really free.

For me, network marketing has been the most viable vehicle to reach financial freedom. I believe it's the average person's ticket to true freedom and the opportunity to actually own oneself.

If you have just been introduced to network marketing, this book will help you internalize the truth that successful network marketing starts from the inside out, beginning with self-improvement and self-discovery. If you are at the point in your network marketing career where the initial excitement is wearing thin and the commitment has become a painful process, this book will restore your energy and revitalize you. Regardless at what stage, this book will:

- Teach you how to identify and achieve your dreams through network marketing

- Support and encourage you through the ups and downs of this crazy business

- Take the mystery out of making it to the top

Some of you may be asking, "At what point did your financial freedom begin?" Well, to be honest my story is not a rags to riches tale. I wasn't on the street, unemployed or destitute. Some might have thought I had it all: I taught at a university, had a lot of time off and experienced an average amount of satisfaction through my job, but for me it wasn't enough.

My dream to achieve more came through the simple invitation of a colleague. She didn't stop to judge whether I would be interested. She didn't wait until she was successful in her own right, or until she was wearing just the right suit and offering the invitation in the perfect surroundings. She just walked right up and asked me if I would like to make some additional income during the summer in a sideline business. I said, "yes". That was my opportunity. There are times I wish I could tell her what a change she made in my life.

At first, network marketing meant a little extra money in the summer; after a while it became the source of a good percentage of my income. However, it was more than the money that drove me; it was an emotional thing. I enjoyed the enthusiasm, excitement and genuine encouragement so prevalent in that positive environment. Looking back on the years I have spent in network marketing, I realize that I have had a fulfilling life. I have risen to the top of every network marketing company with which I have been involved.

I am financially secure. I have traveled the world and done it in style.

There is a saying, "Learn from the people who are where you want to be." Look at the mentors you have now, if any, and compare them with the successful people you see at the top of network marketing companies. Who has more financial freedom, more control over their lives, more exotic holidays, material gains and more time with family? Who lives in a more positive environment and experiences more personal growth? Through my experiences with network marketing, I believe I'm living my life to its fullest. I am grateful to the person who introduced me to the industry.

What I want to do for you is take you beyond where you are now. I want to help you hit the ground running. I have written this book because I believe anyone can be successful in network marketing. All you need is someone to make it simple enough to understand, help you believe in yourself and teach you the tenacity to overcome the disappointments. You don't have to develop your business one little step at a time; instead, you can grow by leaps and bounds. You just have to be willing to take that first step. With this book, maybe I can help you believe in yourself enough to try, work with you long enough to make you stay and coach you until you reach the top, at which point, you will turn to me and say, "You're right my friend, there is no price too great to pay for the privilege of owning yourself."

Paula Pritchard

CHAPTER 1
The Bigger Picture

This book won't persuade you that network marketing is your gateway to easy success. And it won't finish with a little "rah-rah go-get-'um" pep talk. If that's what you are looking for—guess what? Wrong book, wrong business! Network marketing demands a lot, but it gives a lot in return. It's about making the most of yourself and your business. AND SO, my story begins.

The Invitation

Once upon a time I had a real job. In fact, my formal background was college teaching. It was while I was teaching at Kent State University, that I was introduced to network marketing. One day a colleague of mine, a fellow professor, asked me if I'd like to make some additional income during the summer in a sideline business. I said, "Yes," and she invited me to a presentation.

The Presentation

As I look back on that presentation, there were about ten people there and I was the only guest except for two friends I had brought with me. I didn't know it at the time, but that's always been a great lesson for me. No one made me feel like the focus of the presentation, which would have, in turn, made me feel very uncomfortable. No one prejudged me as to my ability or desires; after all, I was young and inexperienced.

And Then...

Who would guess that in four years I would become the first single woman in that company to reach one of the company's highest positions, called

Diamond—and, that I would do it in record time! Because of that accomplishment, I was on the front page of a national magazine, invited with a group of select Diamonds to a White House reception and dinner with the president, recognized in company magazines, asked to be the main presenter at numerous speaking engagements, mentioned in two books (one a national best seller) and awarded many trips—including the company's coveted yacht excursion.

The Learning Curve

What most people do not know is that for the first fifteen months of that four-year trek to Diamond I was unsuccessful, made little money and contemplated quitting numerous times. The focus of this book is to teach you the difference between what I did the first fifteen months versus the next thirty-three months of that four year journey. I made some major changes and learned some life-altering lessons. The best thing to remember about the learning curve is that you will have one, and given the time, you will get through it.

I experienced three major things that contributed to my fifteen-month learning curve. First of all, I kept trying to reinvent the wheel. I guess it was the teacher in me, always trying to find a better way to do something instead of just following the previously proven method. When I saw people who joined after me move ahead of me, I really became discouraged. I finally realized what separated us. They were doing as they were told and I was complicating everything. It was at that point that I realized my sponsor or upline had no reason to mislead me. After all, their success was based on helping me succeed. It was time for me to stop resisting and just have blind faith. It was time for me to believe in and trust in the company and my upline.

Secondly, I was over committed to my job—certainly more than eight hours per day. Can you believe that for a mere $15,000 per year, they owned me? There's a saying, "Some of us are so busy making a living we don't have time to make any money." That was me to a tee.

The third reason I had such a long learning curve was the fact that network marketing was just plain hard when I first began. It wasn't the traditional way of doing business nor did it have the acceptance it does today. Most people thought of it as a part-time sideline business, or even a hobby, and that is exactly how I tended to work it.

A Student of Network Marketing

Although everyone experiences a learning curve in network marketing, for some of us it's a lot longer than others. For me it was fifteen months. The best thing to do is to accept and work through that curve as quickly as possible. Be encouraged! At least in network marketing you can earn while you learn.

When I went to college to earn a bachelor's degree and then a masters degree, it took five years. I had to pay for my education, pay for my books and lodging and sacrifice five years of earning potential. Most people don't give it a second thought since the whole college experience is thought to be a normal progression in preparation for a job. But in network marketing, we have other standards of expectation.

I had a gentleman once say to me, "Paula, I'm going to give it six months. If after six months I'm not making $10,000 per month, I quit!"

I asked him, "How long have you been at your job?"

"Fourteen years," he replied.

"Are you making $10,000 per month at your job?" I asked.

He said, "No."

"You've given that job fourteen years and it still hasn't worked, yet you're only going to give network marketing six months? Come on!"

What's the difference in being a student of network marketing and a college student? In network marketing you determine the length of the learning curve and it can be a lot less than four years. If you put in the time and apply what you learn, I believe you have an opportunity to more than make up for any low earnings you may have received during the learning curve.

The Eye Opener

When I finally reached my fifteenth month in network marketing, I was pretty burned out. I was discouraged more than I wanted to admit. However, just about the time I thought I could stand no more, I experienced several events that turned things around for me.

I was in one of those less than entertaining staff meetings at Kent State University. To my surprise, they announced that one of my colleagues had just finished her Ph.D. Since I was in the middle of obtaining mine, I understood the dedication and hard work it had required. When the accomplishment was announced, the staff clapped. It wasn't a red-handed, tired shoulders kind of clap, but more like a polite, seated at the opera clap. My reaction was quite different. I started to stand up to hoot n' holler, until I realized this was not a network marketing meeting. It was the real world, and what a difference I was seeing. Don't get me wrong; it is not that they were rude. They just weren't truly excited and definitely not enthusiastic. I know my thinking was a bit cynical, but had it been a college football game and someone had just scored the winning touchdown, I'm sure my enthusiasm would have been quite appropriate. My enthusiasm died when they also announced that my colleague would be receiving an additional $1,500/yr raise. I thought, "$1,500! I could make that working extremely part time in my network marketing business, without having to spend all that time and money on a Ph.D." How depressing!

Seeking Sustenance

The 15 months of trial and error were like being in network marketing prison, but every event I would attend and every positive presentation I would hear was a personal reprieve. It was as if we were partners in Monopoly and my network marketing friends had just given me a "get out of jail free" card. The encouraging spirit of network marketing people definitely kept me in the business for those frustrating 15 months. It was time for me to make my move.

Compare—Choose—Commit

Remember the old adage "You learn from the people who are where you want to be." When I compared my mentors at Kent State University with my mentor in network marketing there was absolutely no comparison. At Kent State, they were barely making a living. In network marketing, my mentor had all the material rewards anyone could want such as: a beautiful home, pool, Rolls Royce, motor home and exotic holidays. But success is more than just material rewards. He also had more control over his life.

On one occasion, he took his daughter to Disney World on the spur of the moment to celebrate her birthday. He managed to do what I wanted to do — live a truly free existence.

That's when I decided to take the business seriously. I became an outstanding network marketing student, probably driving him crazy in the interim. I'm sure if you could look back at old slides of awards banquets or national conferences, there I'd be, hanging over my mentor's shoulder with my trusty tape recorder. I taped and memorized every word. Sometimes I only got one sentence that applied to the business, but it didn't matter because I knew one line could change my life.

I'd Rather Switch Than Fight

While I was busy being a student and developing my own organization, I experienced another setback, another turning point! I had tried to reach a goal and hardly anyone in my group participated. I was so angry and disappointed. It was the last straw; I had just had enough. At that point my life changed. My mentor said to me (one of those one-sentence moments), "Paula, if your group doesn't excite you, you've got the wrong group!"

Now, you have to understand, that was the last thing I wanted to hear. I'd just spent 15 very trying months getting this group together and now he was telling me it was the wrong one? I was so disheartened. I actually considered giving up. I seriously thought of quitting the business. I knew I was either going to have to quit or start over. And I didn't know if I had it in me to start over again.

Eventually I came to the conclusion that I could not live as a quitter so I decided to start again. But this time I knew I had to be different. I had to adopt a different attitude. While it was true that I needed people, I realized I didn't need any particular person. So, I decided I was going to completely start over, regardless of whether anyone followed me. I adopted the slogan, "If it's to be, it's up to me!" I knew if things were going to change, I had to change. If things were going to get better, I had to get better. I took full responsibility and left myself no outs. I became 100 percent committed. I was going to make it to the top or die trying, but I wasn't going to quit!

Time for an Attitude Adjustment

Napoleon Hill once said, "Whatever the mind can conceive and believe it can achieve." I recognized right away the value of putting success in my mind as if I had already achieved it. If I was the president of the Chase Manhattan Bank, I would act and dress like the president. My whole persona would be that of Ms. Chase Manhattan herself. This attitude change made a huge difference and caused me to adopt a posture of success.

As a result of this change in attitude, I started to attract successful people who wanted this opportunity and my business took off by leaps and bounds. People saw that I was serious and committed. I would say to them, "I am going to the top, I want you to go with me, I believe we would be good together but either way I am still going." They realized that I was committed to going to the top with or without them. It's interesting how the fear of loss, fear of being left behind can motivate people to action. They want to follow a leader. People want to follow people who know where they're going. No one wants to be a part of someone's test. The secret for me was strength of commitment. Here I was looking for the secret to success and all along that secret was within me, and I never thought to look there. What power the human spirit possesses!

Confront and Conquer

To change, I had to identify my strengths and my weaknesses. One of my bigggest weaknesses was fear. An interesting thing—fear! You can't see it, but it's so real and it can paralyze people and keep them from accomplishing all their goals in life. My mentor once said that fear is "False Evidence Appearing Real." The more I thought about what he said, the more I realized that I was spending a great deal of time being afraid and worrying about things that were, most likely, never going to happen. In the process of worrying about the negatives that may happen tomorrow, I was missing out on all the positives that were going on today.

I once read that a person is born with only two fears: the fear of falling and the fear of loud noises. The rest of the fears we attach to ourselves like barnacles collected on the outside of an old ship's hull as we sail through life. The more we sail, the more we build up all these fears until they eat away at us and inhibit our progress. Once we realize the barnacles of fear are there, we have a choice to peel them off. It's a wonderful feeling to eliminate the extra baggage and take back control of our lives. I used to do a lot of self-talk and say, "Come on Paula. Real fear would be living in a war zone, worse yet, being the soldier in a war zone or coming face to face with a grizzly bear. How can you be afraid of a mere telephone?"

Telephone fear was a constant up-hill battle for me. There were days when the phone weighed 10 tons and I had the fortitude of a gnat in a hurricane. I had to make a game of it. I would make just picking up the phone and making the call a success. It didn't matter if they said yes or no, for me what meant success was that I had faced my fear and picked up the phone. One call, one victory. Two calls, two victories. I was building a history of success in my mind. How light that phone became with all those successes behind me!

Once I conquered my telephone fear, I decided to wage war on all my fears, one by one. After all, fear was what was standing between success and me. So, the next big fear was that of rejection. This was unbelievably hard to get under control until I came to a realization: I was not the issue! If people said "no" it was to the business, not to me personally. I learned to make "no" a part of my trip to success. I stopped turning a three second disappointment into a three week depression. The reality is, "no" and "yes" are part of all businesses, and the more you understand this the more you'll value them both. Eventually you will realize that no and yes answers are equal. You are not bad enough to get all nos and you are not good enough to get all yeses. The only difference between you and those at the top is that they have heard more nos.

Have you ever walked into a retail store, looked around, and then walked out without buying anything? Sure you have! Did you hear a loud thud from behind as the owner collapsed from disappointment? Of course not! Why? They understand the numbers. They know out of so many "no" answers, there are so many "yes" answers. Why do you think storeowners move to high traffic locations, like malls? To get more nos and as a result they'll get more yeses. Go for the "nos". Understand the numbers. Real estate people do, and so do most salespeople. They know how many times they need to show a house to get a serious buyer.

One of the most powerful fears is the fear of what others will think. This is a foolish fear, but real, just the same. If you search long enough, you'll always find people who will criticize your actions. So, why search at all. Good or bad, people will ridicule those who travel an unconventional path, yet most successful leaders do just that.

When I first started network marketing, other people's opinions were very important to me; consequently, I avoided family members or friends who I thought would say, "Have you lost your mind?" or "When are you going to get a real job?" Everyone has an opinion about your decision, and they are more than willing to share it with you if you let them.

Understand that most of the advice they're going to give you will be negative in order to keep you in mediocrity. Keep in mind, no one in your neighborhood is going to run out in the street and cheer you on to build your business so you can move out of that terrible neighborhood. Think of it this way, if you move out and they're left behind, it's a reflection that in some way they haven't been as successful. And if they tell you to get involved in network marketing and you fail, then they would feel like it was their fault. It's much safer for them if they tell you not to get involved and then if you succeed, they can say it was just luck.

I helped myself overcome this fear and the tendency to listen to all the negative comments by simply making a conscious decision not to ask for or listen to unwanted advice. The accolades and respect I wanted most were from those people who were most successful in my network marketing company. In order to win their respect, I needed to work through my fears and do the same things day in and day out to build my business that they did to build theirs. In turn, I would win their respect.

When you look at the people you spend your time with, you really have just a couple of alternatives. Jim Rohn, the philosopher, tells us to look at the people we spend a great deal of time with and ask ourselves "What are they doing to me and is that okay?" If the answers to those two questions are negative ones, then we really only have two choices. Either we don't spend as much time with them as we used to, or we disassociate with them altogether.

The great thing about network marketers is that they are great dreamers and encourage one another to do their best. It's common for those at the top to give positive support and encouragement to face fear head on. Most of them know exactly what you are going through because they've been in the same position themselves. They know that when you identify your fears, you are well on your way to conquering them! Once you conquer your fears, building a team of associates is merely a matter of understanding the numbers.

For Your Statistical Satisfaction

In college I attended a statistics course. The professor talked about how statistics was a real, accurate and predictable science. He then explained election polls and the Neilson ratings. He then explained the "law of averages," one of the major Laws of the Universe, which pertains to numbers. This information was eye-opening as I realized how it could apply to my network marketing business and guarantee my success. By merely applying a certain number of exposures of the business to my formula, being emotionally detached from the answer, I could be successful. I started calculating my exposure ratios. In network marketing, everyone's ratios vary. If you are contacting warm market or referrals, your ratio could be one yes for every three to five contacts. If it's over one in five, you may need to be fine-tuned by your upline. It could be that the problem is technique or belief. Don't worry, either one is solvable. If the issue is credibility, you may need some guidance on working cold-market (people who are strangers to you). If it is belief, that can be corrected too, and through a change in perception, practice and conviction, your ratio should eventually be one in three.

When I was introduced to the concept of numbers and ratios I immediately applied them to my business. I realized that even though I could not make someone successful, sheer numbers would mean that there would be successes in my business anyway, irrelevant of my influence. Keep in mind, the only thing you control is how many people you talk to. You do not control who wants to see the business nor who gets in. And the best part was that, because I controlled the number of people to whom I talked, I could control the numbers. Based on the number of lines my company required to get to the top, I knew exactly how many people I needed to talk to in order to end up with the necessary number to show and sponsor.

Let me simplify further. There are ratios involving the number of people you talk to and the percentage of that number that actually want more information. Then, there are ratios between the number of people you show the business to and the percentage of that number that actually sign in. Finally, there are ratios between the number of people who sign in to the business and the percentage of that number that actually do something.

At the time, I was dealing in warm market and referrals and my ratios were 1:5. That meant that for every five people I talked to, 1 wanted to know more and for every five that I showed the business to, one got involved. That also meant that for every five that got involved, one actually built a business. Eventually as I got more confident my ratios improved to 1:3. If I needed five key lines, I'd sponsor 15-25. That meant I needed to show 45-125 and talk to 135-625. Spread out over 6-12 months, it isn't as hard as it may appear. That way, based on my ratios, five were likely to make it.

Knowledge of the numbers and a willingness to work the numbers put me in control of my business. I knew exactly what I had to do. No more guess work.

Let me give you an example. Suppose you want to reach your goal in about six months. If you take 625 people divided by six months, you end up with 104 people per month or three plus people per day to talk to. Do you think you could talk to three people per day? You really don't even need to mention your business. Be on a fact-finding mission and try to determine what they want in life that your business could help them achieve. Then you file the information away for later use, for a second contact. We'll talk more about that in a later chapter.

Usually the income from five key lines more than compensates for the effort required. If you understand numbers, it helps you to better design an effective plan of action. The discouragement in network marketing comes when your expectations are unrealistic and you lack the understanding of how important it is to hang in there and let the numbers work for you.

I Don't Want a JOB, I Want a Business!

In the early days of my network marketing career, I thought I had no control. I didn't understand how to make the numbers work for me. The mistake I had made initially was that I thought I needed certain people and I was dependent on them for my success. Even though I could control how many people I talked to, I couldn't control who got involved. And I certainly couldn't make them successful unless they wanted to be successful, although I tried.

It is clear now what I was doing wrong those first 15 months. If I needed five lines to reach a goal, then I'd sponsor five people and pray they'd do it. I spent my time motivating them, encouraging them and being immediately available, always at their beck and call. It was awful. I was miserable. I felt like I had a **JOB**!

Eventually I learned the concept that you need people but not any particular person. I also learned that you could not control what they did – you could only control what you did. You control how many people you contact. The number of people that decide to see the business and decide to get involved is out of your hands. You don't control that (hard sell, coaxing, convincing and arm-twisting aside). You only control how many you contact.

Once I understood that, it was time to start over with my group. I would work with those who deserved it not demanded it. If I needed five key lines, I'd sponsor 15-25. That way, five were bound to make it and I, in turn, would be in control. I'd work with the ones who motivated me. Now I came from a point of strength not weakness. People knew I was going to the top with or without them. I was not arrogant, but I was confident – big difference. Keep in mind, if you have to convince people to get involved, you're going to have to convince them to do something once they join. I personally didn't have the time or the energy, and I certainly didn't need the **JOB**!

Don't Try—DO

Like I explained earlier, I adopted an attitude of do or die. I told people, "I am going to the top. I'd like you to go with me. I know we would be great together but either way, I'm still going". In a short period of time, new people started to sign into the business with me and old distributors started to come alive. It was as if they were afraid I was going to make it and they'd be left behind. There was no doubt in their mind or mine that with or without them, I was still going to the top.

People want to know you're sold first. I had to make my commitment first. A wishy-washy "Maybe I'll try it" is like trying to ice skate with only one foot on the ice and one foot on the ground. If you are unwilling to fall, you're only going to go so far. But if you venture out, experience the falls and continue to get up, not only will you become a good skater, but also you'll experience unexpected surprises along the way. You will gain competence that will lead to confidence. You'll gain self-respect and the respect of your peers. Your legs will get stronger and maybe you'll even learn to laugh at yourself and have some fun!

Just remember, it's not how many times you fall but how many times you get up that makes the difference between success and failure. Just look at little failures as stepping-stones on your journey. Remember, as I said before, the only difference between you and those at the top is that they have heard more nos. It is all in the price we pay and the way we think.

In There for the Duration

The stronger you get, the less difficult network marketing becomes. It's really a very simple business. It's not easy; you have to work at it, but what you need to learn is simple. Success doesn't come from something you say or do in one day. It is commitment to a day-in-day-out program that you consistently follow. How well you learn it is a prerequisite for how well you will teach it. You need to be more than a student ... you need to be a teacher.

This brings us to the key point in network marketing success—**duplication**. Everything you do should be duplicatable. For example, don't expect the people you sponsor to do what you are not doing. Don't make the job look too difficult or too complicated, otherwise people will think themselves incapable of achieving your position or higher. If you present the business opportunity and you dress in a $500 suit, rent the most luxurious hotel spot in town, have food catered in and give a "dog and pony" presentation, your guests may love the product but they will, most likely, never join your organization if they think they have to do what you did. As they leave the meeting that evening, they'll probably be thinking about all the money it will take to make a presentation, or all the time it would take to learn to be as good as you.

It's very important to avoid the extremes during your presentation. Believe me when I tell you, it is much better to make networking look so easy that your guests leave with the feeling of "I could do that, and I could do it much better!" One advantage of doing business today is the ability to present the business at home on a three way call, by conference call or on the Internet. This creates a more level playing field for everyone because it is more affordable than renting offices and hotel meeting rooms.

Your success is based on helping other people succeed so your system of success must be simple to follow, easy to teach and most important, duplicatable. Make sure what you're doing is what you want duplicated or, for heaven's sake, don't do it!

Network Marketers Are People with a Purpose

What is your reason or purpose for becoming involved in network marketing? It's something you must constantly keep in focus. Without it you'll drift. For some it's money, for others it's recognition and for many others it may be the freedom network marketing offers. A driving force for me, in the beginning, was personal development. I wanted to become better. Network marketing does that. **It challenges you to grow and become a better person, to learn about yourself and push yourself to the limits of emotion.**

Do Yourself a Favor—ENJOY!

Network marketing will bring many rewards to your life, the least of which will be material. For me the rewards have been numerous: financial independence, the ability to retire if I so desire, a home in paradise in Florida, the car of my dreams and a luxury motor coach. I have been able to travel the world.

Life has been really good, but one of the most rewarding events for me was when a friend and distributor, Laura Carter-Maddocks, with whom I shared the business, made it to the top. At the time I introduced her to my business, her bank had recommended she file bankruptcy and Laura was frantic to find a solution. Since that is what network marketing is all about, helping people find solutions, my focus became that of helping Laura make network marketing work for her. And she did. In less than two years she was recognized in one of London, England's top newspapers as one of the "Top 100 Women Earners" in the entire United Kingdom. She was number 70, and I was so proud! That experience superseded the money for me.

Oliver Wendell Holmes once said, "The greatest thing in this world is not so much where we are, but in what direction we are moving." Follow the principles presented in this book and make your direction all the way to the top!

CHAPTER 2
In the Beginning…

There was a time in our history from 1921 to 1931 when department stores were banned. It was believed that they negatively affected the small-business owner. In 1959 franchising was under severe attack because of its unorthodox way of doing business. Today it is a thriving business model. Network marketing experienced the same scrutiny and in 1976 won its case against the FTC. Today it is a $50 billion business in North America and $100 billion business worldwide.

What Is Network Marketing, Anyway?

Network marketing is a word-of-mouth referral method of distribution that depends on a team of people who tell the company story in order to move products. There are no jobbers, no middlemen, no wholesalers and no advertising costs. Products are bought directly by the distributor from the company and then marketed to the end users, so you've eliminated time-consuming steps and enormous expense. Many times the company is the actual manufacturer, other times the company deals directly with the manufacturer. In still other cases the company provides services that the distributor will market to consumers. It's a wonderful concept.

You have the opportunity to allow others to deal directly with the company as well. This relationship is called sponsoring. You sponsor them so, just like you, they have the opportunity to earn as much money as they like, even more than you if they work hard enough. For helping others succeed, you receive compensation in the form of commissions from the company. They pay you commissions on the volume of goods and services moved by your team of distributors. In fact, the company will pay you a portion of the company's profits for helping them to expand their distribution and distribution force.

The beauty of network marketing is its geometric growth. Success is not dependent upon one person selling a lot. Rather, it's dependent on a lot of people consistently selling a little. It's a tiered system illustrated by the following little anecdote:

A number of years ago, someone asked me, "Paula, would you rather have $30,000 a month or one penny doubled every day for thirty days?"

Well, I'm no fool, I picked the $30,000. In reality, a penny doubled every day for 30 days grows to over $5,000,000. If you doubled it for 31 days, it comes to over $10,000,000.

When you enter the business, you do not have to understand every detail. After all, it's what our financial industry is built on, geometric or exponential growth. Take a pencil to it. If you sponsor one person a month, every month for 12 months, and you taught that one person how to sponsor one a month, every month for 12 months, at the end of the year, you'd have 4,096 people in your business. Or, if you sponsored five people and each of those five people only sponsored five people, this means that all you would have in your first level would be five. On your second level there would be 25. If each of those sponsored five, on your third level there would be 125 people. If each of those sponsored five, your fourth level would have 625. If each of those sponsored five, your fifth level would have 3,125. You'd have over 4,000 people in your business within the first five levels removed from you.

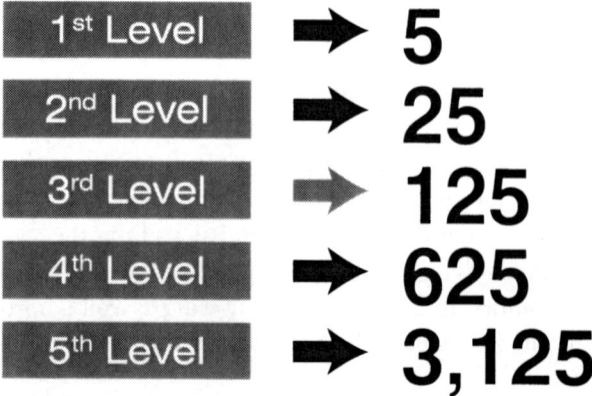

If you keep on working, telling people about your product and business, the rest will take care of itself. It is like telling a story. To become a storyteller is really quite simple. You tell the story about your company and product. If people like your story they either buy and or become involved in your business. Sometimes they're not interested in either, but that's okay, too. You never want to convince anyone to get involved because then you'd have to convince him or her to do something, and that's work. Don't make this a **JOB**! Instead, just become a storyteller.

The better the story, the better your chances are of getting the vision across to your listener. If your listener catches the vision, he or she will soon catch the fever to join in the business and become a storyteller just like you. And, as your business grows, so will your dollars.

Okay, let's see how the money grows geometrically. What if each of those 3,905 people in the earlier example were only producing $100 a month in volume? That's simple—they could do $100 a month just in personal consumption if the company you chose made products that were used in every day living. Well, that means that you'd have $390,500 in volume moving through your business within five levels. WOW!

Now let's talk about the individual. Success in network marketing has a great deal to do with one's own personal vision, the ability to translate the vision into a great story and finally, the number of times that story is shared. For example, you may say to a listener, "Here is my company. Here is the business. Isn't it great?" (Okay, so you'd add some details here and there.) Based on your story, the listener decides:

a) they like the business opportunity and want to get involved,
b) they're not interested in the business, but would like the product as a retail customer, or
c) they're not interested in either.

If you didn't notice, two out of three possible decisions are in your favor. Whatever the outcome, your next thought should be one of the most productive words in network marketing, **NEXT**. After each presentation, you should always think—**NEXT**. What do I mean by that? Do not get depressed if your listener doesn't want to use your product or get involved with your business. You did what you were supposed to do; you told the story. If you told a good story but did not get the results you wanted, you are wasting your time if you allow yourself to wallow in self-pity. Likewise, if every time you succeed in getting someone involved in your business you interrupt your momentum by rewarding yourself with a week off, your business will be like riding a roller coaster. To make your business grow at a steady pace you must quickly move on to the **NEXT** person who needs to hear your story.

The difference in the level of success between one network marketer and another is in the frequency of exposures. Keep in mind, success in network marketing is not in the sell, it's in the show. **Success is the number of times you tell the story or show the business.** All that can come out of your mouth is what is in your head. Consequently, if you have a teeny-weenie vision about your company and product, you will tell a teeny-weenie story. If you have a great big vision, you will tell a great big story. Your story is only as big as the vision in your head. The more powerful and exciting the story, the greater the chance you have of that person seeing the same vision.

A few years ago I was showing a business to a gentleman and he said, "You know this sounds just like the business somebody else was telling me about." Then he paused and said, "No, it couldn't be the same. He was just selling security alarms."

Surprise! I knew it was the same business; I just had a bigger vision, a better and bigger story and much greater results. The difference is the first distributor had a teeny-weenie vision of the company. To him, he was only selling security systems. What a disservice he had done to the company, which really produced high-tech, state-of-the-art consumer electronic products, including: security, communication, education, entertainment, and skincare electronics. He failed to give the big picture when he told his story. Consequently, I sponsored the gentleman and he became one of my top producers.

Did I make my story as big as my vision? I make it a practice to constantly use descriptive adjectives to create a visual picture and make my story an interesting and exciting one to tell and hear. I mean, if my story just said that I sold "electronics," I could be selling wall plugs for all anyone knows, right? And wall plugs aren't going to knock anyone's socks off, unless of course they're sticking something metal inside one!

What Network Marketing Is Not!

Network marketing is not direct sales. A direct sales business is based on selling a product, idea or concept. The most critical issue is individual production. A salesperson must always be concerned about how much he or she is selling and how those volume figures compare with industry standards, company expectations and other sales associates within and outside of the company. Results: sometimes satisfying — sometimes isolating! You see, there can only be one "king" per territory. And, what are the rewards for this sales king? For doing such a great job, they often experience peer resentment, burnout and short-lived positive attitudes, as company executives raise next month's quotas to equal that of its highest producers. Or, the company will split the territories and expect the same results with half the potential buyers.

A direct sales business is production based, constantly concerned with what you can sell all by yourself. It is linear income, addition rather than geometric. You sell; you make money. You don't sell; you don't make money. There are only so many waking hours in a day and your challenge is to figure out how to fill them all with revenue generating activities. The salespeople are constantly looking to climb the ladder of success. It's an upward progression (or often times an upward aggression) toward higher levels of achievement and greater promised rewards. Unfortunately, the rewards are usually not proportional to the work, and reaching that next level is more of disillusionment than accomplishment.

Sometimes it's even a race to beat the biological clock, with the older sales hounds trying to prove they can be just as productive as the younger pups nipping at their heels.

Unlike network marketing, in direct sales there is little time for personal growth and introspection. A balance between personal life and business activities is rarely achieved. A pause on the climb could cause the salesperson to lose his or her place on the ladder. If the salesperson is a highly successful climber, the climb itself becomes so exciting and consuming that home life pales in comparison. Years later, at the pinnacle of their climb, these individuals find themselves going home to Mr. or Mrs. Profit and Loss and spending another satisfying weekend straightening the briefcase and dry-cleaning the business suits.

Network marketing is not a franchise. One of the main differences between franchising and network marketing is the amount of up-front money needed before you can open your doors for business. Most franchises require overhead, inventory and employees. Network marketing invites everyone to participate, with very little initial investment. I believe franchising paved the way for network marketing because it encouraged a more universal acceptance of non-traditional business. So, "hats off" to franchising for doing their part for network marketing.

Network marketing is definitely not a pyramid! First of all, pyramid business schemes are just that, schemes—illegal entities that serve to fatten the pockets of their creators. Although network marketing structures resemble a pyramid, so does the structure of your government, churches, schools and corporations. In reality a good network marketing business resembles a diamond. Here are the three main elements of a pyramid business:

1. Product is either non-existent or irrelevant

2. People are paid for recruiting

3. You can't out earn the person above you

They create an extremely wide base of poor to mediocre businesses in order to support those "fat cats" at the top.

Nothing could be further from the way real network marketing works. It is really the opposite on all three counts. Product is a very important part of our business, since we are paid on sold volume. We are not paid for recruiting and the money isn't taken from one to give to another. The company pays us for helping them to expand their business. The payment is taken from company profits not personal profits. Most importantly, you can go all the way to the top, surpassing your sponsors and everyone in your upline. Network marketing is more like a ladder system. It is just as wide at the top as it is at the bottom. The person that introduced you might be on the second rung, willing to help you to their level, but you can also pass them up at any time. In network marketing, like many other large organizations: churches, corporations and schools, the structure is similar but the business practices are much different.

Network Marketing Means Different Things to Different People

I have had some people in my organization who are very happy making $500 a month, while still others set their sights on making $5,000 per month. Then, I have others who would be disappointed if this month's figures only totaled $10,000. For some, success can be easily transferred to dollar amounts, but to others it's all about freedom, control, independence and having lots of fun with exciting and successful people! They're in love with network marketing and just happen to be paid well for doing what they love. I always tell associates in my organization, when you know what people want, what successful living means to them, then you have the information you need for an effective invitation to look at the business. When that happens and you focus on helping others, you're on your way to achieving your own success!

Network Marketing Puts You in the Driver's Seat

As a network marketer, you are the CEO of your own company. You determine how many hours a week you will work, how many weeks a year you will take off for vacations, how much Christmas bonus you will receive and how quickly you will expand your business. Network marketing will eventually give you more flexibility, independence and control than any other business, but it takes a fair share of patience and commitment on your part.

Why is it that people will allow themselves a lifetime to climb that corporate ladder to success, but limit themselves to mere months "trying" to successfully develop a network marketing business? We'll address some of these issues in Chapter 8, as we talk about how to begin to build a business. The thing to remember is that **you make it happen**! The following is a simple list of dos and don'ts that will help to keep you on track:

Do:

- Look at others who have succeeded in your network marketing business. Ask yourself if they have what you want. If the answer is yes, the next logical step is to follow their lead.

- Attend meetings, listen to conference calls, participate in online presentations, read positive books, listen to training audios and make sure you have the necessary knowledge and tools as you travel the road to success.

- Treat your newly formed business like a real business, and allow yourself the time it takes to build a successful new career in network marketing.

- Work through the practical lessons in this book. It will give you added insight down the road.

- Feel free to go upline for help. The more successful you are the more successful your upline is. This is a team effort.

Don't:

- Seek approval or advice from people who may not fully understand network marketing. Talk to the experts instead.

- Say you're going to give this new network marketing career a "try." Commit yourself to a do or die, all-out effort to achieve success and accomplish your goals. If you treat it like a hobby it will pay like a hobby.

- Expect miracles in the first month or two of network marketing. Think of this part of your career as your freshman year in network marketing college, and recognize the fact that you have a ways to go before you graduate with honors.

- Take mistakes or small setbacks personally. Turn them into learning experiences to be shared with your new network marketing team.

- Listen to negative stories or beliefs about your business. They are usually formed through inaccurate information and offered by individuals whose mistaken motives keep you from achieving your dreams.

- Underestimate the value of your journey and experiences in helping others.

Interesting Statistics

Remember I told you that success in network marketing begins from the inside out? Did you know that 99% of people by the age of 11 years old have a well-defined inferiority complex? In order to live happier and more productive lives, we have to deliberately change. Only about 4% of us attempt to bring about significant changes in our lives. Out of the 4%, only 5% are successful in their attempt. What does this have to do with network marketing? Plenty! All your fears and feelings of inferiority stand in the way of your success and your ability to achieve. If you're not operating at full-speed, how can you develop a business and teach others to reach their full potential?

Here's another interesting fact. All of our lives we are told what to do. As a child our parents give us direction. They tell us what to wear, how to choose our friends and what to watch on TV. Then it's time for high school and we think we know it all. Our parents have probably long since given up telling us what to do, so we immediately think we are free. Wrong! Now we have advisors telling us what classes to take, teachers telling us how to plan our futures and little bells herding us from one room to another.

Finally, the moment we have been waiting for arrives — college. We're all on our own, perhaps many miles from home and authority. Wait, not free yet! We have professors from whom we want to take certain classes, but their schedules dictate when and where we can do that. We have house or dorm curfews telling us when to be in at night. We have curriculum requirements dictating how many classes we will take and when we can graduate. We just can't wait to be in the working world and do exactly as we please, right? Not yet!

In the working world we have to wait for approval for our annual vacation schedule. Some people punch a time clock, which dictates the exact moment to begin and end their working day. Get the picture?

Now here's the catch! Finally you get involved in network marketing. You are in business for yourself with no one to tell you what to do. Instead of freedom, you may experience instant panic! You have been conditioned and told all your life what to do. Now you are in business for yourself with no one to tell you what to do and you are paralyzed. If you have a good sponsor and an excellent upline, they'll help you through this stage. However, what if your upline isn't providing the necessary support to help you achieve your goals? Remember, your direct sponsor is not your boss; he or she is your advisor.

If the person who sponsored you is not doing their job, move through your upline until you find someone who is interested in helping you succeed. Don't think you are putting them out—their continued success depends on your success, and they understand the numbers. Approximately 96% of the population needs to be told what to do. Studies have shown that only 3% of us can work on our own, with just a little supervision. And amazingly, only 1% can work independently without supervision. Network marketing realizes these figures, and has structured an industry that allows you to **work for yourself but not by yourself.**

Did you know that almost 90% of our education is based on facts and figures? This leaves a small 10% that relates to feelings and attitudes. Yet 90% of our ability to succeed is based upon feelings and attitudes. Your success is dependent upon your ability to identify your strengths and weaknesses and your willingness to work on yourself to improve those weaknesses.

Another important factor in creating a successful network marketing business is the ability to choose those who make up your organization. You don't have to worry about whether you will get along with the people you work with because you act as your own personnel service, selecting the people with whom you will be doing business each day. In corporate America, statistics show that over 98% of the people who are fired lose their jobs because they could not get along with their fellow workers or superiors. They know their job, they are qualified to handle their position, but they can't make it socially.

Being social is mandatory in network marketing. If you are short on social skills when you come into the business, you'll soon be made to feel comfortable by the other people in the organization. That is the nature of network marketing. But you'll need to make a concentrated effort to work on your ability to communicate. There are books, CDs, seminars and people to help you. Through this process you also have the opportunity to develop confidence and a positive attitude, overcome your fears and believe in yourself.

Following the Path of Least Resistance

If you're like me, you were taught that hard work paid off in the long run. The harder we worked the greater our rewards, right? In fact, the "American Dream" is based on Average Joe making it to the top due to his dedication, honesty and hard work. While that may have been true for some, today's reality shows that people are working harder and making less. When I was in traditional business, I used to get discouraged when I felt I just couldn't get ahead. It's always disheartening to hear that you've been slaving for years at a dead-end job in the hopes of owning your little piece of cement on 5th and Main, only to discover your neighbors, who learned to work smarter not harder, were enjoying the cool breezes blowing across the verandahs of their beach front properties in paradise.

The reason I wasn't living my dreams was that I was allowing myself to be pulled down by the voices of mediocrity. Don't let this happen to you. No matter how logical the advice seems, if it separates you from your dreams, it's bad advice. What if the Wright brothers had believed all the brilliant scientists and mathematicians who said human flight was impossible? Overnight priority mail would be that which could be hand-delivered after a long night's walk. And, we'd all be stumbling around in the dark if Edison had given up after only 10,000 attempts experimenting with the possibility that we could discover and control the power of electricity!

We in network marketing have learned to keep the faith. We take turns telling our stories, delivering the message of success and sharing in the successes of those we help. It's not a secret club or private party. Network marketers enthusiastically invite everyone to join in and share the rewards of this incredible business.

CHAPTER 3
A License to Dream

As children we have an amazing dream machine. Sometimes we forget but when we were children we could tell you what we were going to do when we grew up, who we were going to marry, how many children we would have, their names and gender, the house we would live in and the vacations we would take, especially those vacations to Disney World. We even had tea parties without real tea. But when we became adults, it is almost as if the dream machine had been broken. Somewhere along the way reality set in and we realized we couldn't have everything we wanted. Maybe it was the invasion of the dream stealers or maybe just our own lack of self-confidence but somewhere along the way we need to get it back and we need to make sure we contribute to the nourishment of our own children's dreams and imagination.

Dreaming Is a Serious Business

The real world doesn't take dreams seriously. Even in school, dreaming had a negative connotation when the teacher would abruptly startle you by telling you to stop daydreaming. In any case, network marketing people realize that your dream is the destination while your goals are the steps it takes to get you there. However, this is quite different from the thinking in traditional business. Many motivational sales trainers for traditional businesses are fond of allowing time in their hands-on workshops to set short and long-term goals. When I would attend such seminars, it always amazed me how people could quickly get to work making their lists of goals. Meanwhile, there I was laboring over writing down just one simple little goal, and that happened only when I was most inspired. So, what made it such a painstaking process for me to set goals?

I Leaned to the Right

The reason I had such a difficult time setting goals was because I leaned to the right — right side of the brain, that is. We have two hemispheres in the brain, with, in most cases, one side being dominant. The right side of the brain houses all our passion, emotion, creativity, imagination and dreams. People who are considered to be right-brained, include: artists, inventors, writers and entertainers, to name just a few. I think good network marketing people should be added to the list. They have learned the value and importance of dreaming.

Left-brained individuals are more analytical, sequential thinkers, like: mathematicians, computer analysts, doctors and engineers. While lefties are in their element setting goals, dreaming is one of their most difficult tasks. Dreaming requires them to step out of their comfort zones. If it is just as difficult for you to dream as it was for me to set goals, here are a few suggestions. Adopt the dreams of others you aspire to be like; after all, it's not likely those dreams have been patented. Take the dreams that sound particularly attractive and make them your own. Usually the people you most admire and enjoy spending time with will have dreams that suit you because their likes are similar to yours. Don't worry, you'll get better with practice; your dream machine is just temporarily out of order!

Who are the Dream Stealers?

For one, we are! We are our own worst enemy! Adults who were encouraged to set aside their dreams, unfortunately, teach their children to do the same. How? Through language and by example! For instance, when children get a little older and they want a bike, or they want a new computer or perhaps they want to enroll in a study course in Spain, what do many adults do? The first words out of their mouths are "Well, who do you think is going to pay for it? I'm not paying for it."

What we should be saying is: "What a great idea. Let's start thinking of ways you can afford to pay for it," which would encourage the child to go to work on solutions and ways to reach their goals in life. Instead, we often take away their dreams because of financial limitations.

We do the same thing to ourselves. We may want a new home or new car, but we look at our income and resign ourselves to deferring the dream.

Maybe we can redecorate with new carpeting and new doors on the kitchen cabinets, rather than going for our dream of buying a new home. Instead of that new car, maybe we'll make the "Rolls Canarly" work one more year. You know that car that rolls down one hill and can hardly make it up the next. We are taught by example to search for ways to modify our dreams to fit our incomes, instead of increasing our incomes to encompass our dreams.

Then there is the language of self-talk, which we allow to steal our dreams. Your mind relates best to your own voice, so what are you saying to yourself? If you tell yourself enough times that you are a good-for-nothing dreamer, then you will fulfill your own expectations and become what you believe. However, if you enthusiastically believe in your dreams and encourage yourself, your chance of achieving them is significantly strengthened. You become empowered with faith in your abilities and it makes you try harder. Over time you will exceed your expectations. When you have a history of exceeding expectations, you are more likely to continue in that vein. You know what they say about history repeating itself. Network marketing operates under the same principles, forming a spiral of success that reaches up and out to limitless proportions.

Change Your Attitude—Change Your Ability to Dream

Wouldn't it be nice if the messages we received all day were positive ones? What if you woke up every morning to an alarm that said, "Rise and shine my friend." Think about all the new uses we could find for that robotic car voice. Instead of hearing, "Your door is ajar," you'd hear a cheery voice say, "My, aren't you looking fine today" or, "You can achieve anything you set your mind to today." By the time you got to your appointment, you'd be feeling on top of the world.

We couldn't help but be successful if we were fed a constant diet of positive reinforcement. Network marketing does deliver that message of encouragement through the daily contact with positive people who have accomplished their dreams. It's the message of success! You can't control what you say to yourself and you can control who you spend time with, so take control, value yourself, protect yourself and choose wisely.

A Dream Permit

We did promise you a license to dream in this chapter, but first you need to get your permit and practice. How do you find out what your dreams really are? Ask yourself this: if your world were a perfect place, what would it contain and what position would you hold? To answer these questions you have to just kick back and let yourself go. Don't worry about how unrealistic or unattainable your dreams seem. When you dreamed as a child, you didn't stop to say, "Wait a minute, there is no need for me to imagine I can drive when I can't reach the pedals or see over the steering-wheel"? No, you just had fun with the dream, right? That's how you should feel now. It may help you to know that many network marketing leaders have now exceeded what they once believed to be ridiculous fantasy dreaming.

At the risk of interrupting you easy dreamers, let me speak directly to you bottom-line thinkers who have been taught that dreaming is a waste of time. It's been my experience that nothing could be further from the truth. Since first getting into network marketing, I have dreamed about all kinds of things I wanted. I taped to my refrigerator door a picture of the car I wanted, the motor coach I wanted, the dream home I would someday live in and the exotic trips I would take. I thought about having the freedom to create a business tailor-made to my needs, working the perfect schedule and surrounding myself with great people whom I had carefully selected to accompany me on my road to success. I looked at these dreams every day, and soon they began to take shape, to become my reality.

But for some people, if the going got tough, they would take the picture off the refrigerator. Why? Because they were material wants and easy to change. They were not internalized. Here is the secret. You must internalize your dreams or goals. Goals become internalized when you concentrate on how you will feel when you accomplish them. How will you feel when you are driving that car? How will you feel when you take the keys to that new house, open the door and tell your children to pick their own bedroom? How will it feel when you earn the respect of your peers or the adulation of your organization? Now it becomes emotional. It is much easier to bail on material goals but harder when emotion is involved.

Playing Make-Believe

Imagination also plays an important role in the achievement of your dreams as well. It's not enough to just think about your dreams and hope for the best. You must draw a picture in your mind and visualize a pattern of successful behavior. The following story illustrates the power of visualization:

A college physical education teacher divided his class into three groups hoping to illustrate a point. One group practiced free throws for two hours every day. The second group did nothing but play around for the same two hours. The students in the third group were asked to visualize themselves making successful free-throw shots for those two hours.

At the end of one month, the teacher measured the students' performance, and the results were amazing. The group who did nothing for 10 hours a week increased their performance by zero. The group who actually practiced shooting the free throws, experienced an improvement of 24%. What is interesting is that the students who only visualized making successful free-throws increased their performance by 23%.

Great athletes have known for a long time the positive power of visualization. Before they go for that gold medal record, they picture themselves winning a hundred times over. In fact, the picture is so detailed that they can tell you what colors they are wearing, who else is there with them, what time of the day or night it is and what they are feeling as the gold medal is placed around their neck. Even if the steps up to the platform are their first, the experience is familiar because it has been there in their dreams every day for years.

Achieving the Good Old American Dream

It's our heritage to be visionaries. The founders of our country dreamed of a land where people could work together to achieve their own personal successes. Instead of one person trying to achieve the impossible, people had the support of their friends and neighbors to help them plow, plant and develop the land. Those in network marketing do the same thing. They help you plow through all the things that keep you from success. They teach you to plant the seeds that will bring you a bountiful harvest of hard-working dreamers like yourself. Finally, they help you to develop the business you want to have. I guess you could say that the network marketing concept embraces the "American Dream." Maybe network marketing is even more traditional than people would have us believe.

A Dream Away from Success

Staying focused and steadily moving toward achieving our dreams is what brings us success. The key words here are "focused" and "steady." One of the most outstanding network marketers I have ever known just happens to be my business partner, Kathy Robbins. She uses an analogy to illustrate just what happens when our climb to the top in network marketing isn't steady and focused!

Think of building a business in network marketing as a challenge similar to that of pushing a snowball up and over a hill. You must roll the snowball on the ground, up the hill. Your goal is to reach the top of the hill. If you are like most people, you will work hard for a while and then decide to take a break. When you walk away from your snowball it rolls to the bottom of the hill. So you start again, only this time the snowball has gathered more snow when it rolled back and it is heavier and larger. Perhaps you hit an obstacle and begin to wonder if it is all worth it. You decide to sit down and think about it. You let the ball roll to the bottom again. Each time this happens, starting again is much harder. You need to decide that you are going to the top of the hill and keep a steady, consistent pace. The momentum and pace you develop will help. Finally you reach the top of the hill and your snowball goes over the top and begins to pick up size and speed all by itself. The growth of your business is the same. If you keep a steady pace of growth, soon you will reach critical mass at the top the hill and your business will grow with less effort on your part.

Turning Your Dreams into Workable Goals

Dreams are empty wants without a plan of action. The difficulties come when you don't have a workable plan, and rather than blame your failures on your unwillingness to develop and work your plan — suddenly network marketing becomes the scapegoat! Why is it that people say network marketing doesn't work, when there are hundreds upon thousands who have proven otherwise? Just because one person is not committed to success, doesn't mean network marketing doesn't work! Just because one person has been unsuccessful at designing an effective business plan, doesn't mean network marketing doesn't work. Guess what? **If you work—network marketing will work, too!**

As I said before, I don't think of goals as the end product, but rather the step-by-step process to my end destination. I'm too busy working on my next goal to spend a lot of time celebrating the one I have just achieved. Don't get me wrong, I believe in rewarding myself, but I stay focused on my original dream. You have to be careful with rewards. With no short-term rewards it's almost impossible to continually move forward. On the other hand, with too many rewards you can become distracted from your original purpose.

The difference between success and failure is often a delicate balance of visionary focus (keep the ultimate goal in sight) and distracting celebrations. In fact, leaders in the business have been preaching for years about the dangers of letting little successes make you complacent and rob you of achieving greatness. Believe me when I tell you, it can be tempting after months of hard work to get to that first level in network marketing and cruise for a while on your past successes. What's the end result? It's lost ground and momentum and delayed arrival to your final destination.

Fuel the Fire!

Your network marketing career should begin with discovering your dreams and end with their achievement. It's that success spiral. When you realize what a powerful motivation dreams can be, it becomes a positive and productive tool in building your network marketing business. Find out what motivates YOU, what inspires YOU! Music has always provided inspiration for me. The fictitious boxer Rocky Balboa and I have a lot in common. We're both at the top of our climb, holding our arms up in victory as the *Rocky* theme plays in the background. We may not have reached our end destination, but we're enjoying our climb to the top!

Like Rocky on his road to success, most of us get into network marketing with a fire inside to be successful. Like Kathy says, "When the going gets tough, and it will, you have two choices. You can treat the tough times as if somebody has just poured a bucket of water on that fire and it's out and it's over. Or, you can act as though somebody has just poured a bucket of gasoline on your fire and it's burning hotter and brighter than ever."

So What Is the Result of All This Dreaming?

A great business and positive personal growth, that's what! Like looking back at the marks your mother may have made on a wall as you were growing taller, you'll be able to look back and measure your personal and business growth. Each level of success will leave its mark. In network marketing, you benefit from sharing your dreams and achievements with others so they can learn from your experiences and you from theirs. It's a mutually beneficial exercise, but you've got to have a plan!

As much as most of us love to travel, we wouldn't want to board a plane only to discover the pilots have no idea where they are going, what time they'll get there or if they will have enough fuel to see us to our final destination. It's the same way newcomers to network marketing feel about joining this new venture. If you, their leaders, have no plan of action to achieve your dreams, no goals to keep you on track, no enthusiasm or energy to fuel your business, what direction can you offer others? It's a two-way, give and take means to success. Network marketing leaders need the support and encouragement offered by their associates to continue to do well, and vice versa.

So now, what's the end result? Personal satisfaction in your own achievements, financial rewards that last a lifetime, friendships that bring enjoyment and offer support and the ability to achieve, as a team, what would have been impossible to do alone — that's what you can have in your network marketing business.

CHAPTER 4

The Network Marketing Nitty-Gritty

I have spent the first three chapters giving you most of the "whys" of network marketing. Now, it's time to get to the "hows." In this chapter I'll cover the special structure and vocabulary that is unique to network marketing. Since network marketing has a language all its own, it's important that you first understand terms that are specific to the industry. So, let's spend a few moments identifying and defining unfamiliar network marketing terminology.

Understanding the Lingo

Up to this point I have tried to stay away from typical phraseology like "I'd like to offer you a wonderful opportunity." It smacks of a "sales pitch." Instead, I like to think of myself as the storyteller who was mentioned previously. I'm just here to tell an interesting, informative and perhaps entertaining story that carries an important message for others who choose to benefit from its telling. Once they hear the story, it is up to them to decide whether they wish to try out for one of the leading characters, a supporting role or merely become a member of the audience.

People being presented with an invitation into the business stand to lose, at the worst, an hour of time listening to an idea or concept they have no interest in pursuing. At best, those hearing your story may have a greater vision than you. They may actually be sitting there planning ways to surpass your achievements and go right to the top in the company. That will be just fine with you because their success means greater success for you too. So, let's get down to the nitty-gritty of network marketing!

Since we will be referring to these terms throughout the rest of this book, here are a few words and definitions with which you should become familiar.

Level

This is the distance a person is from you or another distributor in a line of sponsorship. For example, if you are A, and you sponsor B, they are one level away from you. If B sponsors C, C is two levels away from you. If C sponsors D, D is three levels away from you. Another way you will hear this said is D is on your third level. Levels are actual people or distributor ships.

Generation

This is a term used in some compensation plans. In those plans a generation usually begins with or ends with a distributor that has reached a certain monthly qualification or a certain title. A generation can encompass a number of levels. A generation is a title. So if the designation of a generation is the title Executive, and A is an Executive, D is an Executive, G is an Executive, then you have three generations of Executives.

Leg

In network marketing, leg is a word used to identify a person you sponsored and their entire organization. Sometimes we call this "a line." This would represent one "leg." If you sponsored two people, you'd have two separate legs. Two legs let you travel at a much quicker pace and cover a lot more territory. If two legs help you move fast, imagine how quickly your business will grow with five to 15 legs!

Sponsor

This is the person who introduced you to the business and registered you on an application.

Upline

An upline is a series of sponsors, not only yours but your sponsor's sponsor, and their sponsor's sponsor—all the way up to the top of the company.

Downline

These people would be all those you have sponsored, and everyone they sponsored, and so on to infinity. This is also called your organization.

Sideline

Your sideline is people not in your upline or your downline. Someone in your sideline could be sponsored by your sponsor, kind of like a cousin, or he or she could be someone sponsored by a totally different person originating from your sponsor, as long as that individual is not in your upline or downline.

Width

Width represents the number of people you have personally sponsored while depth is how many people they sponsor and their people sponsor. Width goes wide — depth goes deep. Width represents profitability. Depth represents security. Depth creates a business built on bedrock.

How Does Network Marketing Work?

As I said before, there are no middlemen, no jobbers or wholesalers in network marketing. You act as the distributor who buys directly from the company and markets to the end users (your customers). In the process of product movement, you invite others to join your team of distributors and do the same. This is accomplished using one-on-one presentations, informal at-home gatherings, conference calls, the Internet and informational seminars held in local hotels or other large facilities.

How Do You Get Paid?

Later down the road you may be more interested in the personal rewards received from your involvement in this business, but now is probably the time to focus on monetary compensation. Like anyone operating a home-based business, there are many ways to make income, some less obvious than others.

One of the very first ways you will make money in your home-based business is actually through the money you will save. Because you are starting a home-based instead of a traditional business, you will save the costs of leasing expensive office space, the hassles of hiring employees while paying workman's comp and insurance and the headaches of trying to keep everyone happy yet still make a profit.

Another way to make money by saving money is by being a careful bookkeeper. Discovering all the deductions and tax benefits available to you can be a chore, but the pay-off is substantial. Make sure you record mileage expenditures spent on home gatherings like refreshments and set-up costs. Keep track of your inventory and the amount you spend on product and informational materials used in recruitment. Tally all your travel expenditures, including: airline tickets, hotels, food, dry-cleaning, conference rooms, products and promotional gifts and offerings. Make Uncle Sam your financial backer, instead of having his hand in your back pocket all the time. Make sure you have a separate business bank account and credit card.

Of course, network marketing does not pay you to recruit, it pays you to move product. It pays you on volume created over a certain period of time. That's why products are so important in the development of your network marketing business. If you are still in the search for a network marketing company, try to choose a company whose products or services you and your customers will enjoy using and need to reorder frequently.

That's another money saver/maker. By purchasing your network marketing products/services for personal use at wholesale prices, you'll be saving a bundle. As you invite more people to join in your efforts to move product, it is reasonable to believe your product volume ordered from the company will increase proportionately. If you had to depend entirely upon what you alone could achieve, your success would be limited to the number of hours a day you could work. We will touch on payment structure in a later chapter.

The advantage to network marketing is that you are flanked by many others working alongside of you. You cannot become a leader in the industry without helping others to be just as, if not more, successful than yourself. Network marketing allows anyone to spiral to the top by expanding their businesses outward and downward, building width and depth in their organization. It is an incredibly unique experience, having the opportunity to surpass leaders in the industry and, in fact, being encouraged to out perform them. I don't know too many other businesses where the janitor could become the CEO of the company.

Building Your Company by Investing in Your Dreams

No business, including network marketing, develops immediately and without sacrifices. Like any other endeavor worth pursuing, you have to allow yourself to experience the "learning curve." I've been in network marketing for more than 25 years, but I made next to nothing for the first 15 months in the business. I wouldn't exactly call that an over-night success. Too bad I didn't invest a dollar for every mistake I made; if I had, my fortune would be into the billions by now. But, network marketers are lucky! In later chapters, you'll learn how you are paid even when you are not successful with a particular contact.

One of the best business investments you will make in network marketing is the time spent helping others to achieve their dreams, too. The success of your business goes hand-in-hand with that of those you sponsor, so investing in their welfare comes back to you many times over. Helping others to learn more about the company and the products you represent also helps you to sharpen your skills. It is a fact that people remember only about 10% of what they hear, 30% of what they see and hear, but almost 90% of what they teach to others. Your presentation skills will improve as you teach your downline to be good presenters. You will become a better bookkeeper as you help others to be organized in their business. In fact, your downline will be made up of people whose different strengths can benefit the entire organization.

Incentives and residual incomes are common commodities in network marketing. If you have done an effective job at building your business, you will never have to worry about paid vacations, income lost due to illness or even shortages during your golden years, when you should be out enjoying life. Not only will your upline and downline support you while you are actively participating in the business, but the financial compensation continues for a lifetime. Residual income is like royalty income when someone writes a book, screenplay or song. It is income that continues long after you stop working.

It is the golden goose of network marketing. No more worry about corporate lay-offs, downsizing or struggling through poor economic times. Network marketing allows you to take advantage of pooled resources and team efforts. If your main concern is inviting others to join your organization, supporting their efforts and celebrating their successes, you'll have more job security and financial freedom than you ever dreamed possible.

But, Who Signs My Check?

You do! You control how much money you make in this business. You are paid for product movement, so even using the product becomes an income generating strategy. Isn't it phenomenal to think that you are paid to use the products of your own business? No kidding! Proctor & Gamble doesn't pay their employees to brush with Crest or do their dishes with Palmolive. Isn't it amazing to think that you can promote your skin care line, your nutritional products or Internet product and services by simply purchasing and using the products/services?

You are also paid for teaching and developing others. The sooner you learn to focus on building your business by building those you carefully selected to participate in your organization, the more money will come your way. Network marketing isn't a give and take business, it's a give and give business. By practicing the principles and philosophies of what has created this incredible business, you are developing a strong chain of givers that offer side-by-side support and encouragement. I often have people ask me, "Paula, how many people are under you?" I say, "No one's under me unless I am standing in a cemetery!"

Once when I was asked how many people were in my organization, I said "I am supported and encouraged, and I support and encourage, countless numbers of exciting and enthusiastic entrepreneurs that span 15 countries and represent the movement of millions of dollars worth of product. Our numbers cannot be contained in any executive board room, and our combined achievements outweigh those of any international CEO."

One important tip: if you are making judgments about who will be successful and who won't, save yourself the time. I will promise you this—the ones you think will do it probably won't, and the ones you think won't do it probably will. Don't ever get carried away thinking any particular person will be a star. You're only setting yourself up for a fall. Give it time and nurturing because only time will tell.

I have done seminars all over the world and the experience of unrealistic expectations is universal. You never know who will succeed in network marketing. In fact, I have had people ask me "Paula, how do you know if someone will be successful?" The truth of the matter is you don't! It's too bad they don't have green earlobes or obvious characteristics that make them stand out in a crowd. I guess you have to go back to that **blind faith** again.

Remember, it's a numbers game. In any case, don't spin your wheels looking for that special someone with the look of a top performer because you'll be disappointed every time. Just keep on telling your story, make it good enough to attract those potential high-level producers and you'll achieve your dreams. Everyone wins!

CHAPTER 5
Skills Needed to Be Successful

There is no question that a positive attitude plays a major role in your success in any endeavor. In network marketing it is critical. Staying up beat, positive and grateful will take you all the way to the finish line. That positive energy and expectation of good people and good things to come will increase your energy vibration and enhance your ability to draw positive people to you.

Initially I never understood the reason to work on my attitude, focus on the positive and avoid negative people. When I started network marketing, I started with a blind faith. If my successful mentors told me it was important then I believed them. I nurtured my attitude. I read positive books and listened to positive CDs. I grew in optimism and perseverance. And these are two of the major qualities of winners according to Brian Tracy.

We are so lucky to live in a country where self-improvement books and CDs are available in every bookstore. Just as we would protect our children from negative influences, we need to protect ourselves as well. If you feed the negative all the time, that is exactly what you become: a negative person. It's your choice! If you wish to be positive, then you need to read, listen and watch positive, uplifting things.

Understanding the Importance of Attitude

Whether positive or negative, attitude has a profound affect on your ability to achieve. So, if you won't embark on a mission to improve your attitude simply because you have a personal desire to do so, you may want to consider the affect attitude is having on your performance. If you sit around all the time feeling sorry for yourself, telling yourself you'll never succeed—guess what? You'll fulfill your own prophecy.

For some of you, that picture is a bit too extreme. Maybe your belief system is just a bit shaky. You don't really beat yourself up; most of the time you TRY to be positive and you HOPE you can achieve success. Do me a favor. Take a look at those words and you tell me if they sound like a person who believes he or she has what it takes to become a top producer. They are tentative words, and there is no power in being tentative. Let me give you a little analogy that will illustrate exactly what I mean. If you collapsed with a heart attack, do you want help from the person who says, "I'll **try** to get an ambulance!" or "I **hope** to get an ambulance?" Or, would you want help from the person who said, "I'll get an ambulance!"? Demonstrate your power in the words you use.

You're in Control—It's Your Choice

Speaking of power! Doesn't that phrase give you a feeling of power? Just think—you are in total control of what you think and how you feel. After I entered network marketing and spent fifteen months being frustrated I learned that if I changed my attitude, I would thereby change my results. It was then that I adopted a "do or die" attitude. It is just such an attitude that I believe is one of the major keys to success in this business. It's much easier to hear the first "no" and fold by telling yourself network marketing just didn't work for you. However, before you throw in the towel you have to ask yourself "Why didn't network marketing work for me? Why is it that thousands of people are making incredible incomes and living fulfilling lives through network marketing, and I'm not? What makes them able to do it and not me?"

Are those top-level networkers any smarter than you? Some are — some aren't! Are they more privileged than you? Some are — some aren't! Are they more skilled or naturally talented than you? Some are — some aren't! So what! All those things don't really matter. What matters most is their relentless determination to succeed. They have chosen to adopt a "do or die" attitude.

Give Yourself No Way Out

It's time to accept the responsibility for your own performance and take action to improve it. The first thing you must do is make a pact with yourself. No matter what, you will leave yourself no way out. You will not blame other people or circumstances for your setbacks. Instead you will have the courage to face the negative influences in your life and do what is necessary to overcome their effect on your future.

You'll often hear motivational speakers advise you to avoid the negative. Well, that would be great if it were possible but, in reality, we are bombarded by the negative every day. Removing the negative influences in your life requires more than just ignoring the problem. Getting rid of everything negative is impossible. What you can do is minimize its affect on your personal and business life. How? Make sure you are feeding yourself at least five times more positive than negative. The next time you are tempted to sit down in front of the TV to soak up all that negative programming that floods most channels these days, make a conscious choice to read something on self-improvement instead. The next time you are tempted to blame your lack of achievement on a poor economy, high taxes, the unreasonable demands of others or even the weather, stop and take a look at yourself. If your question is "Why have I not achieved success?" then the answer certainly isn't because success was meant for everyone but you. Maybe you are not ready to make the changes necessary to be truly successful. Nothing is going to change until you are willing to admit that you play a major role in contributing to your own success or failure. Once you gain insight into improving yourself, your business will improve. Make a conscious effort to sidestep negative influence and negative input.

Take a Personal Inventory and Work on Self-Improvement

Jim Rohn, a well known public speaker and philosopher, says that those who are really successful work harder on themselves than they do on their businesses. If I had worked on myself as hard as I did building my business that first fifteen months, I would not have continued to make the same mistakes. It suddenly occurred to me that if I expected my business to change and grow, then I needed to change and grow right along with it.

Don't stop working and sit around listening to CDs and reading self-improvement or motivational books all day. Read a little, listen a little and practice a lot of what you learn. In order to turn theory into reality, you have to practice each new learning step until it becomes second nature to you. Even before that, you have to recognize just what is holding you back. What do you do well and what do you need to improve? First things first, let's take a personal inventory of your strengths and weaknesses.

When I first started network marketing, I had desire and was ambitious, but I didn't have the best people skills in the world. I was easy to get along with, but for some reason I had a hard time looking people in the eye when I talked to them. I'm sure it was the result of a poor self-image on my part. Once I realized that this was a problem, and that it was rude and inconsiderate to not look in the eyes of those I was talking to, I decided to do something about it. I enrolled in a course called "Adventures in Attitudes," where the instructor actually taught me how to look someone in the eye. I discovered that by looking others in the eye as I made conversation with them, they felt important. It was one of the best things I could have learned. Eye contact is essential. I now enjoy the feeling of communicating through eye contact and letting people know how important they are to me and how much I value what they have to say.

It sounds simple, but I believe that that one little thing, not being able to confidently look people in the eye, reinforced the lack of confidence I had in myself. Since we have learned to associate timidity, lack of self-confidence and in some cases dishonesty, with the inability to look in the eyes of others, what kind of impression do you think I was leaving with those I was trying to recruit into my organization? If I thought so little of myself, how could I expect others to have faith in me and in the opportunity I was presenting to them?

Looking others in the eye was just one way I learned to improve myself and increase the positive results in my network marketing business. The longer I spent working on myself, the more confident I became. The more confident I became, the more I believed in my abilities to achieve. The more I believed in me the more others believed in me. Everyone wants to follow a leader. It wasn't something I did back in the beginning and then stopped doing. Working on self-improvement is a lifelong process with lifelong benefits.

My challenge to you is that you begin to take inventory of your strengths and weaknesses. Don't beat yourself up for your weaknesses and don't become enamored with your strengths. Instead, use your strengths to build your self-confidence when you discover some weaknesses that tend to pull you down. When you have identified your weaknesses, make a point to work on those things and make them your strengths. It doesn't mean you will ever feel as good about doing those things as you do the ones that have never been a problem for you, but at least you won't be avoiding them and losing business in the meantime.

Everyone has weaknesses. They are what make us human. In fact, most people can relate to you more through your weaknesses than through your strengths. It's human nature to root for the underdog, to cheer the second place team, to sympathize with those who are struggling with some of the same things you find difficult. So, don't be afraid to admit you need to improve in certain areas. It is a fact that others admire the honesty and candid behavior of someone they feel is truly working to be a better person. Nobody likes a know-it-all or one who acts as though they are perfect.

Work on the little things and let the little successes give you confidence to tackle the bigger things. Each victory will not only create good feelings within yourself, but you will inspire others to do the same. If you want those in your organization to be students of self-improvement, lead by example. By recognizing and accepting that you are by no means perfect, you are more able to accept and tolerate the weaknesses of others.

Most of all, know that part of the learning process is learning to overcome temporary setbacks. In fact, that is what separates most highly successful network marketers from those that only experience average results. The true professional gets up when they think they can't. They laugh at themselves when others would die of embarrassment. They feel fearful just like the rest of us, but they do it anyway; they do what it takes to overcome their inhibitions and be top producers. If they can do it—so can you!

Before you read another chapter, make a commitment to take inventory of yourself. Find a place and time where you won't be interrupted and sit down with a tablet to record your strengths and weaknesses. When you have completed your list, look at your strengths and list all the ways they will help you in your business. Anticipate all the success you will have because you have these strengths. Next, take an honest look at your weaknesses. Think about how they will negatively impact your performance. Write those things down as well. Now, think of what you can do to eliminate them. Let me help you out a little.

First, communicate to your upline what you have discovered and ask if they have any suggestions on how you can improve in areas where you need help. If they are doing what they should be doing, they will know self-improvement books or CDs/cassettes that will best suit your particular needs. If not, keep moving up your line of sponsorship until you find a kindred spirit. That's the beauty of network marketing. In the network marketing business, your sponsors are eager to help you to be your best. After all, their incomes depend on the success of your performance. In helping you they help themselves. Just mention you are working to improve a particular trait and you'll soon have more recommended reading and self-improvement CDs than you can imagine. Have fun. Remember, the choice is yours. Make a choice to enjoy the adventure of self-discovery and improvement.

The Better You Feel About Yourself — the Better You Will Feel About Others

Network marketing is a people business. The key to your success in this business is feeling good about others and conveying your positive feelings to them. As you are working on self-improvement, you'll realize a marked improvement in your ability to communicate with others. When most of us think of communications, we think of talking because that is what most of us do when we communicate.

There is another side to communications — listening. I have a friend named Elaine who is a very good conversationalist. When I think about why, I realize it isn't because she talks all the time. Actually, what makes Elaine such a good conversationalist isn't what she says as much as what she doesn't say. Elaine's strength is in knowing how to listen. Elaine has made listening an art and she is a master. She always looks you in the eyes when you are talking. She smiles and laughs at the appropriate time. She leans over in her chair when she thinks you are speaking about something of particular importance. She occasionally asks a question or nods. Elaine is actively involved in the conversation, and most of the time she is actively listening. Even on the telephone, she asks questions often and responds to your comments in a way that lets you know she is really listening.

What is also important about the way Elaine listens is how it makes you feel. I take calls from Elaine, even if I am busy. I always enjoy our talks and come away from our conversations feeling full of energy and enthusiasm. When she does talk, she rarely says anything negative about our mutual friends or acquaintances and she always speaks of the positive things they say about me. Elaine is my listening mentor. She represents what a conversationalist should be: a good listener!

Be Open and Friendly

Okay, so you're getting a little taste of greater self-confidence and an improved outlook on life. The next thing that will happen is people will become attracted to you because of your positive nature. Positive attracts positive. In network marketing, as in life, the more friendly you are the more people gravitate toward you. If you want to look at it from a business perspective, you will be paid for being friendly and talking to people.

If you are introverted, you'll love the change in perception from those around you. Introverted people are often thought of as antisocial. How unfortunate to lose business and leave others with the impression that you don't care for them when in reality it is a self-confidence issue. The more you push yourself to be friendly in everyday situations, the more people will be attracted to you and the easier it will be to communicate about your business.

If poor attitude, poor self-image and a lack of confidence keep you in your house and not out meeting people, the changes that reading this chapter and other self-improvement books will make in both your personal and business relationships will be incredible. It won't be easy, though. You'll have to push yourself to overcome your weaknesses.

Don't take giant steps in the beginning, just take one little step at a time until you feel steady enough for the next step. I promise you will achieve if you believe you can. Look at babies when they are learning to walk. Do they jump up and begin running before they have learned to crawl? Of course not! They pull themselves up one knee at a time, one foot at a time until they are standing. When they finally stand by themselves the look of amazement and happiness is definitely a Kodak moment.

You'll experience that same thrill when you pull yourself up and make yourself talk to someone while standing in line at the grocery store or the movies. Make it your goal to just begin speaking to people; that will be a victory in itself. Talk to people on the golf course. Talk to people at restaurants, in department stores and in bank lines. You don't have to talk about your business. Just practice being friendly and learn to communicate. Make it an adventure.

Keep the Proper Perspective

When you learn to look at network marketing as an adventure, you'll become the explorer. Not only will you explore how to improve yourself and how to increase your business, but you'll begin to appreciate that adventurous spirit in others. Instead of limiting your business, you'll soon be offering the opportunity to many different people whom you may have previously overlooked. You'll realize that there isn't one person who shouldn't at least be given the chance to hear your story and make up their own mind about whether or not it would be for them. Whether they are a corporate CEO, a secretary, a doctor or a janitor, everyone deserves to hear about the possibilities of network marketing.

I remember being called by a telephone solicitor about a product. The person was so positive and energetic; it was contagious. I thought about how wonderful she would be in network marketing. I complimented her on her obvious telephone talents and upbeat persona. I told her I was looking for someone with her talents. I asked her if she was open to examining other opportunities. She asked me what it pertained to and I told her "People development—helping other people learn the people skills that come automatic for you. The benefits include freedom, unlimited income and a positive environment!" I also told her it would take too much time to explain on the telephone. We set a time to meet. She got excited, got involved and did extremely well.

Get Motivated and Motivate Those Around You

Jim Rohn, motivational speaker and philosopher, has a segment in one of his seminars where he talks about the "NOT MUCH" syndrome. It has to do with making a plan for success and then working the plan. I want to tell you about it here because it speaks to those who tend to blame other people or situations for their failures. If you identified with those I spoke of earlier who blamed the government, taxes or even the weather on their lack of achievement, you need to hear what Rohn has to say. It goes something like this:

> **Jim:** "How much do you think lowering taxes will affect your business? NOT MUCH!"

> **Jim:** "How much do you think having a government controlled by Democrats will have on your business? NOT MUCH!"

As soon as Jim begins a series of these "NOT MUCH" questions, the crowd soon chimes in and responds to each question with the words "NOT MUCH." Then he asks the few final questions that carry so much power.

> **Jim:** "If you are unmotivated to work a plan and depend on others to plan for you, how much will you follow their plan?"

> **Audience:** "NOT MUCH!"

> **Jim:** "And, if you don't have a plan and you won't follow someone else's plan, how much do you think your business will grow and prosper?"

> **Audience:** "NOT MUCH!"

Of course it won't. If you are not motivated enough to develop a plan for your business and organize your time so that you can make the best use of it, that is exactly what you can expect from network marketing — NOT MUCH. The first person you need to motivate is yourself. When you do, guess what will stand in your way of success — NOT MUCH!

Be Committed to Taking the Time to Become a Success

Before we leave this chapter, I'd like to be able to tell you exactly how long it will take to get to the top. However, the truth is, there is no way of telling. Some of you may have a fast start. What takes you a week to learn may take someone else a month or perhaps a year. I can promise you one thing, if you don't quit, if you truly believe you can be successful in this business, and if you make plans, set goals and work hard to achieve them, you'll get there.

Network marketing is not a race. Some people have to work a little harder on themselves while they are building their businesses. Some start with more personal and people skills. Some learn the numbers game quicker than others. Some quickly learn to trust their upline. If you look at network marketing as a race, then you leave yourself wide open to the prospect that in a race there has to be a loser and it could be you.

Instead, think of network marketing as a circle of encouragement, a spiral of accomplishment, a ladder of achievement. In the circle everyone is giving your hand a squeeze of encouragement. In the spiral of accomplishment, your downline is spreading down and out. In your ladder of achievement, your upline is extending a helping hand to pull you up to the next rung. There is really no finish, just growth, recognition and the most amazing camaraderie.

CHAPTER 6
I Am Ready To Go — How Do I Get Started?

We've come all this way just to get you ready to begin your new network marketing business. Your first step in getting started is to register with the company, usually in the form of an application. This is merely a formality that allows you to be entered into the computer system, and it is what links you to your sponsor. More importantly, it is the information used to ensure your commissions and bonuses are sent to the proper address. Registration may take place by mail, fax or online.

The Starter Kit

The starter kit, which may have a different name, depending on the company, likely, will contain everything you need to know about the company and its product. You may receive your starter kit from your Sponsor, through the mail or by downloading it online.

One of the keys to having a successful network marketing business is making sure everything you do is duplicatable. It's important that the same holds true for the starter kit. If everyone has the same information in their starter kit, you are assured of it being duplicatable.

The New Distributor Checklist

I suggest that when you sponsor someone you give them or refer them to an online checklist. This is a "don't want to forget" list as you start your business. I like my checklist to consist of one page. If everyone is using this sheet, they're bound to cover the same information with a new person. Here is a sample of a checklist.

NEW DISTRIBUTOR CHECKLIST

Goals

Begin to formulate clear goals for your business by answering the following questions.

1. What do you want? *(income, lifestyle, etc.)*
2. When do you want it?
3. What will you give to get it? *(time, money & energy)*

Things To Do

	Target Date	Completed
Purchase a starter kit & complete application		
Place initial product/service		
Order support materials and literature/CDs/DVDs		
Set up company supplied back-office		
Schedule business planning session with upline		
Order training programs (if available)		
Review training site and archived audio and video trainings		
Install three-way calling & Internet services		
Order business cards		
Schedule distributor training/ upcoming events		
Schedule conference calls		

What You Need

Planner/electronic organizer
Voicemail/answering machine
Portable digital recorder
Computer

This is just a sample list. The list for each company will be different. You will notice at the end of the list under the heading "What You Need" I have listed some basic equipment that is necessary to run a business more efficiently and effectively. You will be amazed at the number of people who do not have these items. These items will change with the changes in technology.

Digital Recorder

This is really a necessity in this business of learning. After all, how will you learn what has made those you admire successful if you don't first hear it, tape it, transcribe it, memorize it and then duplicate it? I mentioned before how persistent I was in taping my mentor in the business when I first started. Actually, I may have been a little more than persistent. I was obsessed with taping. I didn't want to miss one important word. Remember, one sentence is enough to change your life and when it is spoken you don't want to be without your recorder.

Planner/PDA Organizer

Of course, the most logical use for a planner is to keep a daily schedule of all your appointments. I'd like to suggest some different things as well. Purchase a planner with a car mileage log. It's much easier to have it in your planner so that it is with you all the time. Be sure there is a section for frequently called telephone numbers with a space for the results of your last meeting or conversation.

Probably one of the most productive uses of a planner is the ability to list your most important activities for that day. It's a great way to keep your goals in mind and do what it takes on a daily basis to accomplish them. These little daily checklists are a must for me. When I start feeling like it's time for me to stop for the day, I look down at my list. If I have accomplished everything on my list except two things, I'll try that much harder to finish them too. It is a daily form of accomplishment, and it shows you if you are developing any bad habits. For example, if I consistently leave all my calls until I get home and am too tired to return them, I may want to start doing them earlier in the day. If I consistently fail to accomplish everything I set out to do but find that my planner shows little activity until noon every day, I may want to change my start time.

If you get in a rut, your planner will reveal work patterns. If someone in my organization is falling off and cannot identify the cause, I'll often ask them to take a look at his or her planner. It doesn't lie! The night before, sit down and number the most difficult and important things first then set your mind upon their accomplishment above all others. By writing them down the night before, you're burning them into your subconscious mind. This will become an important step in their completion.

Keep in mind, your most important activity is recruiting. Make sure your most important appointments are recruiting appointments, yours first and then your downline's.

Telephone Options

I recommend you get a separate line for your business, preferably not a business line, which costs more. Having a second line will allow you access when you need the phone for business. If you can't afford a second line, you may want to check with the phone company for a custom ring feature to be placed on your regular home phone. For a nominal fee, the company will give you another number and it will ring through on the same line with a different ring. That way you can distinguish between personal and business calls.

Another way to distinguish between personal and business calls would be to order caller ID from your local phone company. This feature tells users the name and number of who is calling. Not only will caller ID help you decide whether or not to take a call, but it is a great way to record who has called you in case they don't leave a message.

There are also various follow-me calling products with one number that will actually ring more than one phone simultaneously. It records the voice of the caller so you can screen calls.

It is necessary to have a three-way calling feature that will allow you and those in your downline who need third-party validation to be on the phone at the same time. You can also use it to connect your upline or simply talk to two distributors at a time. It is relatively inexpensive and gives you the advantage of conferencing with those in your organization who may need training or help. They can learn from one another and you simultaneously.

Call forwarding is another feature that proves valuable when you don't want to miss a call. Make sure that you have some way to screen your calls and pick up your messages when you are out building your networking business.

Voicemail is available in most areas, although some people still prefer to use an answering machine. Both work great. Answering machines give you screening capability. This may not be overly important when you first begin your business, but phones can become an uncontrollable interruption in an otherwise productive day.

I usually let my downline know when it will be convenient for me to accept calls. Of course, in case of an emergency, I always keep my cellular with me. In fact, there is really no reason to be inaccessible these days. Between phones, pagers, mobile phones and computers, there is always a way.

E-mail is sometimes the best method of communication and with e-mail and texting capabilities on our cell phones we are never out of touch. It is great for newsletters and announcements since you can send to everyone in your organization at once. E-mail allows the option to quickly send a note or comment to a number of people at once. My e-mail messages are usually short and to the point, and thereby they save me a lot of time compared to calling each person individually.

Computer Equipment

Your business will be much more organized and easier to manage on computer. If you do not have a computer, it needs to be one of your first purchases. It will help you communicate more effectively with your people. Today we use computers to develop business presentation and training materials, to present the business and to train distributors.

Many people use the computer for recruiting. There are many online recruiting companies who supply leads and online recruiting systems to network marketers. There is also extensive training on how to recruit by visiting various chat rooms and meeting people. In fact, there are some people who have built their business entirely over the Internet.

The downside, for most, is the developing of relationships, which is a vital part of network marketing. Building a relationship online is possible but takes work and time. An important point here is that recruiting people you do not know through Internet leads, ads, chat rooms, etc. takes a special skill set and extra training and is not necessarily duplicatable. Not everyone can do it, so carefully evaluate this method of building and its ramifications and rewards before you start.

Learning Materials

Some of the most important materials you can have are those in your library. You don't have a library? Well, now is the time to begin collecting books and CDs that will teach you, inspire you, encourage you, motivate you and simply entertain you. I realize that many people's lives are just too busy to have time to do a lot of reading, but if you'd just read a few pages a night before you go to bed, you'd be amazed how many books you could read in a year. If the book is available on tape or CD, most people can always find time on a plane, in a car or while exercising to listen to one. Some of my favorite books are *Discover Your Possibilities* by Robert Schuller, *Think and Grow Rich* by Napoleon Hill and *The Power of Positive Thinking* by Norman Vincent Peale. If you want to find excellent reading material, find a book you particularly like and look in the bibliography for a list of related reading materials. Also, ask your sponsor or your upline mentor what they have read that they found stimulating and motivating.

Use Every Product/Service Your Company Offers

How will you be able to tell people what will best suit them if you haven't personally tried every product your company offers? Every business recommends this practice. You wouldn't walk into a McDonald's restaurant only to discover that particular franchisee doesn't carry the Big Mac. Let's say the franchisee had never really tasted the Big Mac but felt it was too expensive for the clientele. How long do you think it would take McDonald's to say "adios" to that franchisee? Waiters sample food to learn what things taste like so that they might best inform their customers. Librarians read books in order to recommend certain authors and their works to people looking for a certain type of writing.

This is one area in which I will advise you not to scrimp. Don't be afraid to invest some money into your business. You won't have a convincing story to tell, you won't move product, and you won't inspire people to join your organization if you are too narrow minded to understand that your company has expanded their lines so that both they and you can reach a wide range of individual preferences. Try them all. Use them all if possible and make them all available to your customers.

The starter kit should be very helpful when learning about your product because it should contain extensive information on all the products. It should also contain a history of the company you have chosen to represent. Use this history or background information to help you in the telling of your story. What's a story? Well, in network marketing it's your description of the company, your vision of the opportunity.

I guess, in some circles, they could call it "a pitch" for slang, but in reality it's much more than that. It is really how you feel about your company and product, and how you envision the opportunity and its future. Give your contact the full picture of the company. Within the history of the company, you should be able to find information that clearly illustrates the company's philosophy and business practices. You should also have some information about the compensation plan. Don't be too concerned with this in the beginning. Your upline sponsor will explain the entire compensation plan to you, and you'll become more comfortable with it as you grow in the company.

Most important, you should have a product list and information about everything available to present to your contacts. Thoroughly get to know the products/services you are distributing. Even though we emphasize the fact that it is important not to inundate your contact with too much information and overwhelm them with your knowledge, you need to know your products/services inside and out. We'll talk about product knowledge and its uses in the next chapter.

The Business Planning Session

After you receive your starter kit, your sponsor should arrange a planning session with you preferably within 48 hours. Understand that there are two opportunities in network marketing. One has to do with marketing the product line only, while the other includes marketing the product line and offering others the opportunity to market the product line. Start to put an action plan together so you have a track to run on. It will be based on what it is you want to achieve.

Marketing the Product Line

Many people entering network marketing have no interest in recruiting; they simply wish to market the product line. Whether part or full-time, a person can make a good income without recruiting. The thing you must remember about marketing the product line is that when you are not selling you are not making money. Eventually you will reach a ceiling on your income. Like a doctor who is limited by the patients he can see in a 24-hour period, or one of McDonald's restaurants that can only sell so many hamburgers in a 24-hour period, you can only sell so much product in a 24-hour time frame. That is why it is important to market a repeat product. If you want larger profits, you have to be willing to let others in on the opportunity with you.

The Opportunity of Company Expansion

The great thing about network marketing is that you can expand your business the same day you start. Isn't that amazing? You can recruit someone else the very day you sign up. Believe it or not, that is a great way to start. Begin the business with a few friends and one of you sign up the other and so on. That way, you can help one another build your businesses. Company expansion, or inviting others to join your organization, opens up limitless opportunities to increase your dollar volume in earned commissions and bonus offerings. Once you begin to build an organization, your income isn't entirely dependent on your own personal efforts. Isn't that great? — residual income!

Remember, this is not an employer/employee relationship. No one makes money out of someone else's pocket. It is also not a hierarchy. I hate it when someone refers to someone else as being under them, almost like a subordinate. In this business we are recruiting others to join us side-by-side in the big race. Who crosses the finish line first still remains to be seen. Only in this race everyone can be a winner. The fastest time is not a part of the equation.

In order for you to fully understand what happens in the planning session, let's take it step-by-step.

Step 1: Explaining the Relationship

Your sponsor should explain the relationship you will enjoy together. Each one of you should be clear about your role in the relationship. Your sponsor's role is to help you plan, organize and understand the business. You bring to the table your **contacts** and the **credibility** you have with those contacts. It should be a mutually respectful relationship. You will have someone to turn to for help. A sponsor who really cares about you and your business will help keep you on purpose. She or he will care enough to tell you to stop your complaining and do what you promised yourself you would do. Remember, this is not an employee/employer relationship. You are both independent contractors in business for yourself but not by yourself.

The time you spend with your sponsor either face to face or by telephone should be productive time in building your business. Listen to your sponsor present each part of the business. Tape the presentations, transcribe and memorize what was said and done, and practice duplicating your sponsor's success. Get so good at doing what they do that the words sound like yours and the activities are second nature to you.

Don't complicate matters by trying to put your own spin on it. Focus on duplicating the people who are where you want to be.

Step 2: Understanding the Compensation and Marketing Plan

You don't need to understand everything, but you do need to know the qualifications that will get you to the next level or position of increased commissions and bonuses. It is important to know that the first 90 days will set the pace for your business and determine its foundation. Take advantage of all the energy and enthusiasm you have your first 90 days in the business. Knowing the marketing plan can help you set your game plan.

Maximize your earning potential by making the most of your beginnings. If you have already been in network marketing more than 90 days and are now reading this book, don't worry. Your 90 days can start anytime, once you make the decision to start. Sometimes we repeat our first 90 days until we get it right. The reason the first 90 days is thought of as the time with the most impact is because it's the time when you have the most contacts and enthusiasm. After all, no one has said "no" yet.

We have a saying in this business that, "ignorance on fire is better than knowledge on ice." So remember you can learn as you go. Just don't lose the excitement.

Step 3: Go Over Your Dreams and Goals with Your Sponsor

One of the most important things you can do right up front is to clearly communicate your dreams and goals to your sponsor. For instance, let's say I recruit three people: one wants to subsidize his or her income by working part-time and making $500 a month, while the other two wish to work full-time making $5,000 and $10,000 per month. If I give them all the same business plan, they will be either overworked and experience burnout or be underpaid and decide this wasn't quite the opportunity they had expected. This is the challenge your sponsor has with you. So he or she needs the specifics on what you want to achieve.

It will be helpful if you make a list of your dreams and goals before you meet with your sponsor. Think about how you would like life to be in five years. Where would you like to live? What type of car would you like to be driving? What would you like to be doing? How would you like to be living each day?

Once you have all your dreams and goals down on paper, evaluate which ones are most important. Then think about which ones network marketing can help you to achieve. One specific goal you must consider is what income you want to be earning in the next twelve months. That will determine how many people you need to talk to and what types of activities you need to be doing to achieve your income goal.

Step 4: Discuss the Development of Your Business

Who would you like your business partners to be? Just as you and your sponsor are working together to develop your business, you will be selecting business associates as well to work with you. Who are you going to let in on this opportunity? How will you contact them?

Step 5: Formulate Your Plan

As you look at the first goal you wish to achieve, discuss with your sponsor how and when you will reach that goal. Let your sponsor know just how much time you can devote to the business during that first 90-day period. If you give your sponsor an honest representation of the time you plan to spend, together you'll be able to set realistic goals and expectations.

Step 6: Schedule 90 Days Out on a Calendar

Network marketing typically runs on a 90-day cycle, so it is wise to schedule yourself accordingly. The following are a few of the things you will want to include on your calendar:

- Distributor training sessions/on and off-line
- Business briefings or business presentations/on and off-line as well as teleconference calls
- Internet presentations by the company if applicable
- Company and distributor events
- Conference calls (on-line or teleconferencing)

Understand that the initial training is critical because knowledge will increase your competence. Competence will increase your confidence, and increased confidence leads to a strong belief. Confidence and belief will make you all-powerful at recruiting and building others. The faster you learn the better. Don't expect to hear the information once and know it. Get a qualified training series that is portable so you can listen to it over and over again. If it is portable you can learn while you drive to and from work, while you are chauffeuring the children or even while exercising. Just make sure the trainers you chose to follow have actually done what they teach. In other words, learn from those who are where you want to be. Learn from people who've been successful.

It is a must to attend or listen to as many events and training sessions as possible your first 90 days in the business. Events can be live presentations, online presentations or conference calls. Participating in events educates and inspires you and your people and gives you and them the bigger picture. Also, events and training sessions keep you updated on any new products/services and how others may be presenting them. Remember when we talked about challenges either fueling your fire or putting it out? Well, attending events, on-line or off-line, helps you to keep the fires of enthusiasm burning. Be sure your downline attends. Success breeds success. Surround yourself and your downline with top producers in your company and have a lot of fun in the process.

Step 7: Placing an Order

You've said what and when you want to achieve your goals, now it's time to place your order so you'll be prepared for your success. You don't need an enormous amount of inventory at first, but I do recommend you keep at least one of each product on hand. Some of you may wish to keep one to use and one to sell, depending on the expense of your product. If you have been involved with marketing product in the past, you'll understand that buying and selling is an emotional business. It's always good to have product on hand to service the "right now" emotional buyer. No one wants to wait for delivery. If your product is a service be sure to place the order for the service as soon as possible.

Like everything else in this business, make sure your business planning session is duplicatable. If you are already registered with a company and have not yet gone through your business planning session, contact your upline sponsor and get the ball rolling. Pay close attention to how it is done and duplicate the planning session so you can help your downline. It may be helpful to observe various upline distributors work through a business planning session so you learn the best method for you. If you tape these sessions, you'll capture every important word.

Timing is critical. Planning sessions should be scheduled within 48 hours after a new person signs into the business. Make sure you adhere to this schedule with your recruits. If too much time passes between sign up and planning session, your recruits could experience buyer's remorse. They'll feel lost and wonder if this was really the right thing for them to do.

Let them know how important their success is to you as they begin their business. Here's a little tip. In a perfect world your sponsor will do all these things within the required time frame. If your sponsor didn't do a good job and you need help in this area, contact someone else in your direct upline. They will be happy to help you. You won't be putting them out; you'll be putting money in their pockets.

When I first started network marketing my sponsor didn't know any more than I did and neither did his sponsor. The next upline was someone I didn't particularly care for and his upline was extremely busy working and traveling to help more successful distributors than I was.

As luck might have it, his upline (five upline from me) was a soft-spoken, gentle, loving man named Harold Miller. Harold worked hard at Goodyear in Akron Ohio, and with his wife Greta and his six children, Harold had his hands full. But, this didn't keep Harold from doing what he knew it would take to be successful. He was at that meeting the night I saw my first network marketing opportunity. Harold was very kind, and he also saw ability in me I hadn't recognized myself. He volunteered to help me build my business and explain the opportunity to others. Little did he know how hard I'd make him work!

I owe a lot of my success to Harold. Not only did he get me started right but he encouraged me and kept me in the business during the difficult times. I actually learned how caring and nurturing network marketing could be through Harold's willingness to help me build my business.

One last word of wisdom! In most cases, you will continue your business just like you begin it. If you begin your network marketing career being attentive to details and thoroughly examining what it will take to make you successful, you'll continue on that path. If you begin by treating it like a hobby where you can dabble and make a few extra bucks a month, most likely that is how you will continue until it dwindles away and you stop altogether.

Furthermore, because people attract like people, you'll attract people just like you. If you work hard and represent your product professionally, so will your organization. If you started with the right amount of product and supplies so will your people. If you started on a shoestring, so will they. You set the example.

Now that you are ready to begin, let's get going! In the next chapter, I'll show you how to select the product line that will suit your individual requirements and give you the maximum marketing opportunities. So, have fun, work hard and achieve your dreams!

CHAPTER 7

What About the Product?

Network marketing companies that experience the most success in this business do so because they have a product that is universal, that anyone could use, that is affordable and fills a need. When we talk about product we are talking about both tangible products and services. Although product is very important to a networking business, it's not only having a quality product that will build your business but also how you feel about your product or service that is important. How you feel about your product makes a difference in how you tell the product story. It makes a difference in the enthusiasm and energy you maintain while building your business. And, it makes a difference in the way other people perceive your satisfaction in your network marketing career. You can have a great product, but if you aren't excited about it, your contacts won't be either.

It's important to share your love for the product/service when recruiting others into your organization. So, when searching for the right product/ service to market, make sure you can speak honestly and enthusiastically about all the benefits it offers. When people get excited about your product/service, it's much easier to get them excited about joining your organization. That's the way you'll build your business.

Believe in Your Product

The single most important thing about selecting a product is that you believe in it. If your company says the product will do something and you have difficulties believing that it will, dump the product. You'll never be able to convince others of something you are not convinced of yourself.

I've seen companies do enormous volume with mediocre products. They never claimed to be the best. They claim to do the job and be affordable. I've seen other companies come out and try to compete with these companies by providing the best, and yet those companies fail miserably. Having the best product doesn't necessarily make the best network marketing company. Many companies with superior products enter the network marketing field and don't make it, usually because the product was not affordable.

If I were you, I'd be more interested in a company that was financially stable, had a great marketing plan, timely, high-quality, and preferably consumable products, professional tools and attractive, informative promotional materials and website. A company that was aggressively staying on the cutting edge of technology, as far as supplying their people with the communication tools to help them get their message out, is one you want to consider.

A company that offers a good, affordable, high-quality product is better than a company that offers the best product but everything else is not in place. Remember, it's a package. Sometimes the company with the best products will price itself right out of the marketplace. After all, there still has to be enough margins to pay a reasonable commission.

Bottom line, believing in your product creates interactive marketing and that is what's going to sell the product.

The Story

The story is crucial. It is essential to have a good story around the product and/or the company. The stronger and more unique your story, the more impact it will have on the listener, increasing their interest in your business.

Is It Possible to Have It All?

You bet. Many network marketing companies are financially stable, have competent management, a great marketing plan and a superior product. Keep in mind, with technology changing so rapidly, it's hard to have the best product for very long. There's always the new and improved version with more bells and whistles. That is why a company with an outstanding research and development team is important.

Are Consumables Really Important?

Absolutely! Consumables (or monthly billable services) will add stability to your business with volume from ongoing distributors and customers who consistently reorder product. Auto ship capabilities enhance the company's income flow and stability. The more you use something, the more you talk about it — or tell your story. A product that can be tucked away for long periods of time on a shelf in your garage or closet is going to be tucked away in your mind as well. Sure, you'll drag it out every now and then and find a little time to tell your story of which you can't remember too well and aren't enthusiastic about any longer. Consumables are the key. Keep your products fresh — use them, talk about them, and continuously work on your story and remember others people's results on them. Be as consumed by them as they are by you!

Use the Product

If you're not sold on the product, how can you convince anyone else to be? You must fall in love with your product. Develop a long-lasting relationship with your product. What sells you on a movie? An excited neighbor or friend says "Wow, what a fantastic movie. Between the special effects, sound and story, it was an incredible experience!" You hear in their language and their enthusiasm that they really liked the movie and you trust their judgment. What are you going to do? Go see the movie the first chance you get.

It is the same with your product. You are empowered if you are excited about the product you are using and promoting. You are a more authentic when you talk about your product if you believe in your product. A personal relationship with a product helps you to anticipate what the customers will ask and how to best address those issues. A great product would be one that you could actually have someone else try without a major demonstration being required. If you could just hand the product to them and let them take it, try it and feel the same results that you feel, it makes building a business so much easier. It's an added plus if it is an emotional product that they already require and not one they have to be educated about.

Network marketing is about you using a product, getting excited about what it did for you and telling another your story. The absolute perfect situation is when you can use your product and allow your prospective customer to either watch you use it or use it themselves. This is **interactive sales** versus **event sales**. An event sale requires you to sit down, explain it, sell it, demonstrate it and then, finally get around to letting them use it. It is not as duplicatable.

The Most Powerful Question in Network Marketing: "What Is That?"

We've talked about you using the product, now let's take it a step further. If possible, make it a point to use the product in public. In fact, make as big a "to do" out of it as you can. When people see what you are doing, they get curious. Make them ask that all important question, "What is that?" This question opens up an opportunity for you to get them interacting with the product. And, by them generating the conversation, you are not a salesperson. You are responding to their question by telling them about your product.

Results Marketing

Network marketing is really just a series of results. You are talking about the results you experienced and the results others have experienced while using your product. That is results marketing. Let your contacts know what other people have experienced when they used the product. That is the best way to sell your product, through third-party endorsements and testimonials. When you talk about what you've experienced and then tell them about what others have experienced, that is verification that the product truly works.

Look at how most products on television are marketed — through third-party endorsements. In other words, a laundry detergent company doesn't just display their product and say "This is what our product will do. Buy it!" Instead, they usually have a person who has used the product say "This product removed the grass stains from Johnny's blue jeans. Now I don't have to worry about letting him go out and play, even after a rainy day!" They are telling you their experience as a user, not as the company.

Sell Personal Benefits Not Product Specifics

People get interested in the product you are offering because of what it will do for them. They don't really care about the special product features or about the specific information or ingredients of the product. Although I must point out that there is more of an exception now than ever before with people promoting green and organic healthy ingredients. But they still want a product that works. They want to know what's in it for them. When you talk to them with excitement and enthusiasm about what someone else experienced when they used the product, you've created a curious interest in the product. You are talking about results that they want. That's what is going to sell it.

One of the most popular lines in network marketing is nutrition and skin care. Obviously, that's not an easy product to carry around, although I have known people who actually carried the nutrition tablets in a container and managed to always make quite a bit of noise with them as they pulled them out of their purses or briefcases at a luncheon. Their goal was to raise the level of curiosity and awareness of all those around them. What does that do? It makes others want to ask, "What is that?" As soon as they do, the storyteller goes to work.

On the other hand, weight loss products are the perfect product. Your product is visible all the time. You display your results by bringing people's attention to the fact that you've lost weight. That can create curiosity. Who wouldn't want to have the results they are seeing you experience? And, it isn't about you telling them — you're showing them your personal results. Now that's powerful.

Again, the best way to market nutrition and skin care products is to talk about results. For example, if you're going out to lunch with a friend, set your vitamin container (assuming it is small) on the table to take your vitamins with your meal. If your product is skin care, pull out your hand cream and put it on your hands sometime during your visit, but don't forget to share it with those at the table with you. Next thing you know, not only do they want some cream of their own, but they are telling everyone else about how well it worked for them. They're networking!

You can also start a conversation that leads to the magic question. For instance, you might discuss the energy you feel since starting to take a new nutrition product or how great your skin feels since you have been using a new skin product. They always ask, "What product is that?" Now you have a captive audience who has **asked** you for information. A network marketer's dream!

Don't Win the Battle and Lose the War!

If you get technical with people, nine chances out of ten you're going to win the battle but lose the war. For instance, if you're trying to sell nutrition products, and you get into all the specifics about what each vitamin does to improve the body, or the specific ingredients in a particular product, you've just lost the war. Why? Well, even though you may convince the contact to buy the product, they will never believe themselves capable of duplicating your level of expertise about every ingredient within the product. The contact will probably even be excited enough to tell a few people about the product, and at best refer them to you. However, they'll never take ownership of the business themselves and actively become a distributor.

Wouldn't it be better to get them involved in the company's opportunity and let them be helping themselves make more profits? If you want to make contacts that will lead to possible distributors, you have to make what you do duplicatable. Make them leave you thinking "Boy, I could do that. I could explain that product." If you're product is a skin care line, it's fairly easy to simply say "My skin has improved 100% since I've been using this new product." However, there are some products that lend themselves to more explanation. That can lead to disaster. Keep it general! I'm sure you've heard of the KISS principle—Keep It Simple Sweetheart! Take it from me — that is good advice for network marketers.

Keep it general. Focus on results and other testimonials. The more simple your presentation the greater your chances are of getting the contact to become a distributor. When someone does try to lead you into a more in-depth discussion of your product, and your product is nutrition, my advice is to say something like this: "I don't know a whole lot about that. All I know is how I feel, and I feel terrific. Let me tell you what's happened to so and so since he's been on the product." Or, "Let me tell you about Jayne's results since she's been on the product. I'm sure you're going to love it. You're going to feel just like Jayne and I do."

Another thing to mention would be the product guarantee since most products do carry a money back guarantee. "You know what, I'm so sure you'll love this product, and if you don't feel the same thing we felt, I'll be more than happy to give you your money back. But, I know you're going to love this product!" Those are easy things to say, nothing technical or difficult.

Think Closet Not Warehouse

You are not the manufacturer! You don't have to warehouse the product. That's another plus about network marketing. Do you need product on hand? My advice would be "Absolutely!" However, it doesn't take a warehouse to handle that "on hand" product; a small closet will do nicely. If you are serious about your business and you want to be successful, then it is important to understand that network marketing products are usually an impulse buy. People want them now; they don't want them three weeks from now.

If you want to take advantage of all your selling opportunities, it is important that you have a few of the products on hand. If you have products that move quite rapidly, then you'll want to make sure that you constantly fill the pipeline. You never want to be caught empty handed without the product available to service that impulsive customer. Get in the habit of watching your inventory. Make sure you've got enough to get you through until the next delivery time. Become a real business owner. Fill the pipeline. Just like McDonald's, product moves in the back and out the front with no gaps. No one comes to McDonald's expecting a brochure.

Services = No Inventory

Some of the most popular products, for this very reason have been services like telephone, paging, cellular and utilities. Think about it. What could be more universal? After all, everyone needs and uses one or more of these services. Because of the enormity of this market, the earning potential is astronomical.

Let me share with you some key phrases that will help you market these products:

"Could you do me a favor?"

"I need your help."

"If I could show you a way to save … would you give it a try?" (Never say switch, it's too permanent.)

"Please."

Create Emotional Involvement

It's a funny thing about excitement and enthusiasm—they're contagious! Nothing will move product faster than an excited distributor. It's easy to feel that way when you use and fall in love with your product. If you feel "so-so" about your product, guess what? So will your contacts. Network marketing is not a ho-hum business. If that is the way you feel about your product, get another product. Your success depends on how good your story is, and how good your story is depends a lot on how you feel about your company and its product. How you feel affects your attitude and determines your believability.

I've known distributors who have been in the business for a long time and have forgotten the importance of what I just said. Their business becomes a real JOB, and their results begin to show that fact. They can have the story down and know everything about the product, but when they lose that spark they lose business. People hear the music not necessarily the words. On the other hand, I've known new recruits who really knew very little about the product and company. They didn't have a good story, but their excitement was incredible and it was easy to tell they were in love with their product. They could hardly contain themselves because they were so excited to tell their friends about their new product.

We refer to this as "ignorance on fire," which in this business is one-hundred times more powerful than "knowledge on ice!" I can't emphasize enough how important it is for you to have fun with this business. Let your prospective clients see that you are having fun and making money also. The world has enough miserable people who hate their jobs and hate their positions in life. Don't be one of them. In fact, give your customers, who may be feeling some of this, an opportunity to get out of the rut that may have trapped them for so long. Pretty soon, you'll have a booming network marketing business!

CHAPTER 8
Building a Distributorship

Building a distributorship with a network marketing company involves developing a business plan. There are a number of steps within this plan. The first is to choose your partners or your associates. The second is to contact those people. Third, show them your business. The fourth is getting those who decide to join you off to a quick start based on a proven success system. Then you will simply continue to repeat this plan of action over and over and over again. I'm going to give you all the specifics in each of these steps so that by the time you finish reading this chapter you will have your plan of action to build a successful distributorship.

Most people come into network marketing with no prior experience in the industry. Therefore, what they bring with them are only experiences from traditional businesses. Some of these experiences are good; some of these experiences are not so good. When people enter network marketing, they enter a whole new way of doing business, and sometimes it's difficult for them to comprehend what this industry is all about. What I like to do is use analogies. I like to relate this business to other businesses of which most people are, perhaps, more familiar.

The Coca Cola Analogy

One analogy I use quite frequently is the comparison of this business to Coca Cola. I do that because I understand the magnitude of this opportunity, and I want to get that potential across to a new person whose understanding is limited. I compare this business to Coca Cola because Coca Cola is an unbelievable success story. I'm sure that most people know that if they had the rights to Coca Cola today, they would be an instant billionaire. I bet if you had the rights to Coca Cola today or the recipe to Coca Cola, you'd be out of your mind with excitement. But, would you have had the same vision in the late 1800s when Coke was first created and wasn't the mega success it is today?

It amazes me sometimes how different people can be. I know that there are some people who could receive the recipe to Coca Cola and immediately be contemplating how much money they could make in their own hometown. While others would be thinking, "How much could we make if we took this throughout North America?" Still others would look at the same opportunity and say, "North America? What small minds! How much could we make if we took it globally?" What is the difference between these three people? I've said it before—it's the six inches between their ears. It's called vision!

There are some people who will look at a tremendous network marketing opportunity and say, "Isn't this a cute business? Look how much I could make in my own neighborhood." Others might look at the same opportunity and only see global possibilities and potential. I believe you will only build a business as big as your vision. If your vision is small, you'll build a small business. If your vision is large, you can build an enormous business.

Because it is hard to know what the future can bring, it might have been hard to envision today's Coca Cola back in the 1800's. Think about it! Who would have imagined that that little container of dark liquid with some CO_2 added to it would become a multi-billion dollar industry? Who could have imagined that someday Coca Cola would be in every household of America, in every service station around the world, in every grocery store and every hotel, every restaurant or that it would be served at every social event, bar-mitzvah and wedding? Imagine being able to find it in these little machines on street corners where you would put in money and a can of Coke would pop right out the bottom.

You Have a Great Opportunity—Be Selective with Your Business Partners

If you had the rights to Coca Cola now, you would be smart enough to realize that you could not take Coca Cola worldwide by yourself. You'd have to be willing to let some other people in on it with you. Let's say that you could only bring on five associates, and those five associates would share in the billions and help you take Coca Cola worldwide. Which five people would you pick? Would you pick your brother-in-law? Would you pick your next-door-neighbor? I don't know about you, but I'd pick the five sharpest people I know — visionaries! I'd choose people who were ambitious and hard working. I would choose people with the right qualifications.

Would you be selective? Would you try to coax and convince those five to join you? I doubt it! In fact, you'd be looking for them to convince you that **they** were qualified, had the same kind of vision and would be an asset to taking this company worldwide. If you were sharing this concept of Coca Cola with someone and they said, "I don't think that Coca Cola will work," would you try to convince them? No way! Have you ever heard the saying "You're only as strong as your weakest link"? That person would definitely be a weak link.

It's the same with network marketing. Why would anyone try to coax and convince others to join their organization? What happens to you and your business when you adopt this demeanor? Well, if you have to coax and convince people to get involved, more than likely you'll have to coax and convince them to do something once they're in your organization. That would be like a job. Look for people like yourself, people who can see opportunity, people who have vision!

By now I'm sure you understand the comparison I'm making. If you are going to build a large network marketing business, you can't do it alone. You must be willing to let some other people in on it with you. Those people, just like the ones in my Coca Cola analogy, will be your partners. They will be people that will run side-by-side with you in building your business. So, make sure you choose wisely. Look for people just like you with enthusiasm, excitement and vision.

Remember, amateurs convince; professionals sort.

Where Do You Find Your Partners?

You may have already thought of some key people that you'd like to bring on as associates. Right off the top of your head, these people come to mind. Stop! Don't contact anyone and don't prejudge anyone. I'll let you in on a secret: one of the biggest mistakes made in network marketing is trying to work from memory. The best advice I can give you is to get a tablet of paper and empty those names and others on the pages of that tablet.

Forget about your particular network marketing business for a while. Just empty your brain. Pretend you are earning a thousand dollars for every name you put on that list. List everyone you know, from the time you were a kid, through everyone you've met on your previous jobs. Include everyone in every neighborhood in which you've lived, fellow students, teachers, counselors and administrators in the schools you've attended. Write down the members of every organization and club you've belonged to in the past or ones in which you currently participate. You should be rich by now with all those thousand dollar bills you'll be paying yourself. Just keep on recording names on that list. You may be saying "Paula, that will take me days." You remember that pretend game of paying you a thousand dollars for every name? Well, it's no game. That list will make you rich!

Don't even think about the network marketing company and who would be good. Just take time to list everyone you've ever known. Don't prejudge and don't exclude anyone, especially not women. Women are great in this business. That's why over 80% of the people in network marketing are women.

I have a friend, Sue Burdick, who's a very strong woman in network marketing. She always uses Ginger Rogers as an example of women's potential. You know, Ginger Rogers did everything that Fred Astaire did only she did it backwards and in high heels.

Network marketing offers an equal opportunity for women. The company's computer pays you based on volume, not on gender, race or nationality. It pays you for what work you do, not who you are.

Is your list filling up that tablet? Good, keep going! Here's a tip. Keep an additional pad in your car. You never know what street, song or landmark will trigger your memory and remind you of someone to put on your list. I realize that on this list there are people you don't like, people with whom you wouldn't want as business associates, people who are three months old, people who are ninety! It doesn't matter! All I want you to do is just empty your brain. Once you've done that, the next step is to categorize the list. We will talk about that next.

This Is the Beginning of Your Distributorship

Now it's time to categorize your names. You'll need a red pen, blue pen and a green pen. By listing everyone that you've ever known, there are probably some names that have reminded you of other people. There may be people not on the list whom you totally forgot about who would be great in a network marketing business. Take some time to revisit your list.

Now, what I want you to do first is take the green pen and check off everyone on the list who is like you, who has vision and ambition. Think of the ones on this list who are always talking about being in business for themselves. This is usually the easiest category because these are the people who are like you. These are the people you enjoy being around because they talk about ideas instead of just people and places. They inspire you.

Some of these people might already be successful. Remember not to prejudge someone because they're successful. If you were in a traditional business would you refuse to head-hunt the competition's successful executives because they were already successful? Would you say, "No I don't want someone who has already proven himself or herself with another company; I'd rather have an inexperienced, needy, down and out person"? Absolutely not! We're not looking for "Needers" — we're looking for "Wanters."

There are really only two options out there. If they are successful, they're either successful working for someone else or they're successful owning their own business and working for themselves. Keep in mind, if they work for someone else, that company is never going to pay them more than it would cost to replace them. If they are in the highest paid employment profession, they probably hold some type of sales position. Traditional sales positions come with some disadvantages attached to them, like quotas that tend to change every year, and territories that sometimes tend to be adjusted as well.

In traditional sales, when someone succeeds, the company motivates them by increasing their quotas or cutting their territory. It appears the company never wants to pay them too much or allow them to be too successful. On the other hand, if they are self-employed, we know that in many cases they'll have overhead, employees and other various headaches. Chances are they'll have Uncle Sam in their back pocket.

Depending on the type of business these people are in, there are always constant changes going on in either technology or new products. Trying to keep up with the competition is tough and extremely stressful. So, if they are successful in either sales or their own business, they probably have the discipline and work ethic to become very successful in network marketing. What I'm saying is don't overlook these people. They may be unaware of other options out there where they could own their own business and yet own themselves at the same time, instead of having the business own them.

Something I always found elusive when I owned my own business was the ability to have both time and money. I could make the money, but I didn't have the time to enjoy it. I used to tell people I owned my own business but, in reality, the business owned me. I wasn't free. I didn't know there was another option. I didn't know I could have time and money, too. I was surprised to hear that in network marketing I could make unlimited income and still have freedom and lifestyle to enjoy it. So, don't prejudge. Take that green pen and check off anyone on that list who is like you.

Next, use the red pen to check off anyone who is dissatisfied with their job. That would include people who hate their jobs, hate who they work for or hate the people with whom they work. They might even dislike where they live. Maybe they were transferred by their company and would prefer to move to another location. You know who these people are because this is what they talk about when they're at social gatherings or business functions. They talk about what they don't like or what they don't want.

Finally, use the blue pen for the third group. This group is people who are "wanters." These are people who aren't really unhappy with their job, but they want more. They wish they had more vacation time. They wish they had a bigger house. Or, maybe they wish they could pay for their children's college education.

All three categories represent "hot" buttons. They represent things that people want, whether it's a new car, a different job, a bigger home or whatever. These are all wants. Later in the chapter I'll show you just how to use this information to get you and your contacts what you both want.

After you have categorized your list, narrow it down to your top ten possibilities. Who are the sharpest ten people that you'd like to have as associates in your business? Then choose your second top ten and your third top ten. Please understand, just because you're identifying them as your top ten doesn't mean they're going to get in the business. Some will and some won't. So what? It doesn't really matter. It doesn't make any difference. Right now, all you're trying to do is identify those key people you want to contact first.

Now I Have to Work Up a Perfect Presentation, Right?

Okay, let's go back to the recipe for Coca Cola. Now that you have the formula, wouldn't you contact the top names on your list and set up a time to sit down and show them the Coca Cola opportunity? Of course you would! It really wouldn't matter what time of the day, where you decided to meet, what the setting was or what you were wearing. The story would be so strong in your mind, and your enthusiasm would be so great about Coca Cola that you could tell the story about Coke anywhere. This is just my point! Why wait to get everything perfect? Sometimes we get so hung up in network marketing on all the artificial things and these outside issues that we forget what is really important — simply telling the story.

As far as I'm concerned, the vision is what needs to be perfect. Once you have the vision and the excitement, you'll have the big picture in your head, so what comes out of your mouth is going to be a big picture. Don't get me wrong. You're going to need to wear a suit on occasions. Try to mimic your contact. Dress the way you think they'll dress so they feel comfortable. Don't ever let them out dress you.

We have a saying that goes like this **"People hear the music; they don't hear the words."** If you maintain your energy and excitement, you'll have the music within you. When you have the music and enthusiasm, the conviction and the vision, people will see that you are committed and that you believe. Again, don't be so crazy or excited that you annoy people instead of interest them, but have a controlled intensity and come across one-hundred percent committed. If they don't see it, they don't see it. Move on! NEXT!

Now going back to the Coca Cola analogy, if you were going to show the Coca Cola opportunity, you would probably show them a can or bottle of Coca Cola. Maybe you'd show them a video or picture of people enjoying the taste of Coke while they were out having fun. This is exactly what you will do in your network marketing company. Show samples and pictures of the product. Every time you show the business, you have a chance for three answers. The great thing about it is that two of the three possible answers are in your favor.

The first answer you could receive is "Yes, I want to get in the business," at which point they'll be able to get the product at wholesale. The second answer could be "No, I don't want to get in the business, but I would like the product," at which point they'll buy the product at retail. The third answer could be "I am not interested in the business, and I don't want the product." See what I mean? At least two of the three possible answers are to your advantage.

What's also great is that you are saving time in your presentation. When you are showing the business, you can be marketing the product at the same time. You're marketing the business even when you are showing the product and vice versa. When people ask you how the product is sold, you say by using it and showing it to other people. And, don't forget to let them in on the fact that it also sells when we show the business.

Delivering the Message

Sharing this business with other people is merely telling a story. You are a storyteller. If you owned Coca Cola, you would be telling the story about Coke at every opportunity. You'd be telling people about its past and your vision of where it was going. When you talk to someone about your network marketing company, you're doing the same thing. You're telling them about its past, what it's done so far and what the future holds. **You're letting them know where you envision it going and what part you want to play in that trip.** Your words are really the tools of the business. They should describe and explain, excite and inspire, and move your contact toward a decision. The more you tell the story, the greater the chances are that some people are going to hear the story, capture the same vision and want to travel the journey with you.

I also tell people that they are a messenger. They are delivering a message of a company and of a vision where they believe that company is going to go. You have to understand the important issue here is the message, not the messenger. You need to work on getting the message right. So many people get hung up on the messenger end of it, and it's really the message that's the issue.

Remember, you are the messenger not the message, the delivery agent not the package, the commercial not the show.

Tips for the Invitation

When you invite someone to see your business, let me give you a tip. I'm a big believer in scripts. I believe they essentially give you a crutch in the beginning. They also help you to get your words right. If you are inviting people to a larger presentation, try to stay away from the word "meeting" because it sounds long and boring. It sounds like PTA. I use instead words like "company briefing" because it sounds brief, or "information seminar" because it sounds informative. For a smaller presentation I use the word "get together." One of my favorite lines that I'll use is "run an idea past you" because it's very casual and comfortable when people think you're just going to run an idea by them. Whether over the phone, over the Internet or face to face, the words you use paint the picture.

So, why use scripts? To help you get your words right. They'll help you paint the right picture.

Leave Them with a Good Impression

It is very important to remember that when you show this business, your main goal is to leave a good impression. And that's it! If they say "no," your answer should always be positive. You don't beat them up. You don't make faces at them. You don't tell them they're stupid. You just wish them success and ask them to keep you in mind should their circumstances change. It doesn't hurt to ask them, "is that no for now or no forever?" If it is just a no for now, ask them if you can stay in touch. Keep in mind there are some people who for very good reasons can't get involved right now. In fact, I knew a gentleman who had just spent a great deal of money starting another business when I shared with him a network marketing opportunity. The timing was just not right. I could not expect him to get excited about my business when he had just made a major financial commitment to his own. I said two very important things to him that left him with a good impression. One, "I want to wish you the greatest success because I know you're going to be really good in your new business. You have what it takes to be successful. If somewhere down the road things change, I want you to think about me because I'd love to work with you." Second, I added, "In the meantime, if you run across anyone who's looking for an opportunity, I hope you'll tell them about me. I'd love to work with them."

I left a good impression. So he was probably thinking, "Boy, she really was professional, and she certainly was nice. I wouldn't hesitate to send anyone to see her because I know she wouldn't embarrass me. She'd be just as nice and professional with them as she was with me."

By saying those two things, you can't believe how many referrals I get. In fact, I have one man who started a business in Toronto. I told him I knew that he would be good at his business because he had what it took. Then I asked him to think about me down the road. A year later he called me up and said, "Hey, remember that business I had? Well, I just sold it and now I'm ready to start that network marketing opportunity with you." Why did he call me? He could have called a number of different people. He knew other people in the business, but he called me because I had left a good impression!

Scripting Is Important

When I start someone in the business, I usually give them a basic script. I believe it will help them. When someone is new and nervous, one of the biggest mistakes they can make is to talk too much. Most people come into this business thinking they have to know all the answers before they can start building; consequently, if they get on the phone and someone starts asking them questions they feel they need to give them all the answers. Sometimes they'll give them answers when they don't even know the answers. They feel they have been put on the spot and they don't want to say they don't know.

Sometimes I just shake my head when I overhear these conversations. In some cases, they get on the phone and begin to make up answers. I've discovered things about my company I didn't even know. Then, when they get off the phone, they're pulling their hair out and saying, "I'll never pick up the phone again. What will I do if that person calls back?" That's why scripts are important. I don't want a new person to have a bad experience.

I want them to have the right words and control the conversation from the very beginning. Most important will be their vision and enthusiasm. We can always fix the words.

I certainly don't want them to make themselves the issue. If they feel as though they have to have all the answers, they delay getting started. When I got started in the business, if someone said "no" to me or asked me a question I didn't know, I felt inadequate. I can't tell you how many times I walked away from that phone or that face-to-face meeting, thinking if I'd just said this differently or did that differently, they would have said "yes!"

That is called the "if onlys" — if only I had worn a different suit, or if only I had shown the business in a fancier office. If only I had told them about this or that—then they would have said "yes!" Let me share something with you. Once I got all of that right, some still said "no" and others still said "yes." What was so liberating was to find out that it wasn't me. Just like it's not you. Isn't that exciting — it's not you!

I have interviewed successful people. An important point is this: when all is said and done, you can't say the wrong thing to the right person or the right thing to the wrong person. They either see it or they don't.

The Invitation

This invitation is designed to keep beginners from talking too much on the phone. It also keeps them from getting in a position where they're asked a lot of questions. There are basically two different types of invitations. I call them the direct approach and the indirect approach.

An important tip is that the person asking the questions controls the conversation. So if asked a question, answer it and then immediately come back with a question.

Direct Approach Script

I'll start with the direct approach because it's the one I use with the beginner. It has four steps:

- Introduction
- Lock-in
- Want
- Close

Step 1: Introduction

This invitation takes about one minute. The introduction sets the stage. It tells the contact you only have a minute and that you're on the run, or that you have an appointment. You start the conversation with "Hi, this is Paula. I've only got a minute. I have to be somewhere." You're setting the stage by letting them know up front that you only have a very short period of time to carry on this conversation. If you preface the conversation this way, then when they ask a question you can always say "Oh, I'd love to get into that in detail, but I have to be somewhere." Don't ever say, "I can't answer" or "I don't want to answer that." Just say, "That's what I want to talk to you about, but I don't have the time to go into that right now."

Never try to explain the whole business in this initial contact. It is a good idea to separate the invitation to hear about the business from the actual presentation. Throwing everything at a contact at once devalues the opportunity and gives the impression you are not really looking for a serious business relationship. I will discuss presenting the business a little later.

Step 2: Want

Now, the second step is the want. If you remember, you categorized your list based on wants and narrowed it down to your top ten. You should know what the want is of the person that you have on the other end of the phone. Remember, they want to quit their job; they want a bigger home; or they want to be in business for themselves. Keep in mind, their "hot button" or "want" is going to make them want to look at your business more than anything else.

An important tip is that people are most interested in themselves. If you want their attention, focus on them.

Some people make the mistake of thinking that money is the key issue. They will contact someone and say, "I found a way for us to make more money or a lot of money." Money by itself doesn't mean anything. It's only when you turn it into something you want that it means something. It's what you buy with the money that counts. So let's say, for example, that the person you're talking to wants a Jaguar. Well, if you say money, then they have to take a lateral step in their thinking process and turn the money into a Jaguar. What if they don't do that? You're leaving it to chance. What if, instead, they turn the money into the electric bill and the electric bill doesn't excite them? If you want someone to look at the business, you call them up and say "Jaguar," and if that is their hot button, they should say when, where and how? Whereas, if you say money, it delays the process and it's only by chance that they might think of a Jaguar. Don't leave anything to chance. Why not just say, "Jaguar" straight out?

Let me take you this far in the introduction so you can get a feel for how it sounds:

> **Paula:** "Hi! Listen, I've only got a moment, but I wanted to ask you something." (Now, here's the want.) "You told me a while back you wanted a Jaguar." (It could be a house or a job, etc …)

Step 3: Lock-in

This is the time you use a lock-in or a commitment question: "Were you serious or kidding around?" You see, most people will not contradict themselves. It's a statement that locks them into their want. They will never say, "I'm serious, but no I don't want to find out how I can get it." When they say "I'm serious," then you go to the close.

Step 4: Close

The close comes right after they say "I'm serious." You immediately say "I think I've found a way you can have it. I can't go into it now. What are you doing later? Let's set an uninterrupted time to talk (or get together if that works). I'd like to run an idea past you."

Keep in mind, the word uninterrupted implies no phones ringing, no TV, no children, etc. It elevates the importance of the time.

Here are all four steps together:

> **Paula:** "Hi, this is Paula. I've only got a moment, but I wanted to ask you something. You told me a while back you wanted a Jaguar. Were you serious or were you just kidding around?"
>
> **Contact:** "I was serious, Paula!"
>
> **Paula:** "Great! I think I've got a way you can have it. I can't go into it now. What are you doing tomorrow? Let's find an uninterrupted time to talk. I'd like to run an idea past you!"

Wasn't that easy? Do you think you could learn that? Sure you could. Let's try it again. Let's say what this person wants out of their job.

Paula: "Hi, this is Paula. I've only got a moment. I've got to be at an appointment, but you told me a while back you wanted out of your job. Were you serious or were you just kidding around?"

Contact: "I was serious."

Paula: "Great. I think I have a way you can get out of it. I can't go into it now. What are you doing tomorrow? Let's set an uninterrupted time to talk. I'd like to run an idea past you!" (Do you think they're going to sleep that night? Probably not because you have added something called anticipation. By delaying the chance of getting together or talking until the next day, you have stimulated their interest.)

As long as you know the person's want, you can fit anything into this. When you use the want, you're hitting on something to get their attention. You definitely have their attention right from the very beginning.

What If You Don't Know Their Want?

If you have a contact on your list, but you didn't put a check by their name because you didn't know their want, here's a way to determine their want. It's called FORM. **F** stands for family. **O** is for occupation. **R** is for recreation. **M** is for message. It's a great way to begin a conversation and find out a person's wants, just by following this simple formula. FORM will work with people you know, people who are slight acquaintances and even with people you don't know.

First let's use it with people you know. Pretend you have someone you would like to recruit. You know them because they're someone you call on in your job. You've talked a lot but never about anything personal. Here's what you are going to do the next time you are with them. Begin a conversation focusing on the FOR part of FORM, family, occupation, recreation. At the same time imagine that you have a file cabinet in your head.

The heading on that file cabinet is "wants." Your goal every time you hear this person say something they want is to file it away until you determine the most powerful "want" for this person. Then that's the "want" you'll use in your invitation.

Assume you're calling on someone with whom you do business. Strike up a conversation about their family, which is the **F** in FORM. Ask if they are married. Do they have children? Do they live close by? In the process of the conversation, you might find out that they live in an apartment and they wish they lived in a house. Or, they may have so many children they would like to have a bigger house. Or, they might tell you that one of their children is almost ready to go off to college. You might say, "That's expensive, isn't it? But, I'm sure you're able to afford it." Then they'll proceed to tell you that they're really not able to afford it, or they wish they could afford it. Try to give them leading questions that will make them tell you the thing that they can't do or would like to do if they had more money.

When you discuss the **O** in FORM and you talk to them about their occupation, always say to them, "You're so good at this. I bet you love it." It's amazing how often you will say that to someone and they will tell you what they hate about the job. If you say you bet they hate it, they'll tell you what they love. People are so funny. So, always talk about them loving what they are doing. Let them give you reasons that they don't love it.

When you get to the **R** in FORM for recreation, ask them what they like to do for fun. Maybe they'll say they like to fish. You might ask them what kind of boat they have. These are leading questions. They might say they don't have a boat but wish they did. You then come back with a question that allows them to share with you what kind of boat they would love to have if they had one.

The **M** in FORM stands for the message. If you are talking to someone you know, don't deliver the message about your business at the same time you are collecting your information. My advice is that you deliver it either later that day or the next morning. Call the person and say, "Hey, I've only got a moment, but I've been thinking about our conversation yesterday. You told me you wanted to send your kids to college, or you told me you hated your job, or you told me you wanted a bigger house, or you told me you wanted a fishing boat." (This depends on the "want" you have selected as the primary "want," the best "hot button" for this person.) Then you say, "Were you serious, or were you just kidding around?" (They say they're serious.) Then say, "I think I've got a way you can have it. I can't go into it now, but I'll be back out in your area next week. Why don't we get together for lunch? I'd love to run an idea past you." It makes them think that the only reason that you called them was because of your prior conversation.

What if You Don't Know the Person?

Now let me give you the scenario for a person you don't know. Where do you meet strangers? You meet them everywhere. You meet them at the doctor's office, in bank lines, grocery lines, even on-line. Let's say you're in a doctor's office and you begin a conversation with someone that you don't know. Maybe you begin talking about this particular doctor. Through that conversation, you might talk to them about where they live. Do they live in this area? Do they have children in the local school system? It is a similar conversation that you had with the person you knew.

You might ask them what they do for a living. No matter what they say they do, even if they dig ditches, you say, "I bet you love it." You would be amazed how many say, "No, I hate it." You want to file away all these "wants" in your head. Then you talk about what they do for fun and how much vacation time they have each year. They might tell you they only get a week off and they can't do anything in a week. You might then ask them what they would do if they had more time off. They might say they like to travel and you'd say, "Me too. Have you ever been to Tahiti or Hawaii?" They might then say, "No, but I'd love to go." These are all "wants." You're talking about family, occupation and recreation. Most people like to talk about themselves if you just ask questions.

Sometimes I even recommend that you do this at every opportunity you have, regardless of whether you deliver the message. You need to practice. I call it scrimmaging. You need to practice talking to people, so that you're comfortable talking about family, occupation and recreation.

The difference with a stranger is if you're going to deliver the message, you need to do it on the spot. Don't leave it to chance. Don't rely on the telephone book to find this person's number. Just wait until the very last minute, when you're about ready to part ways. Use the same direct approach. "Listen, I know we can't talk much longer here because the doctor's calling you (or me) in, but you just said that you hated your job. Were you serious or were you just kidding around?" They will say, "No, I was serious." Then you can say, "I think I might have a way out. (At this point I might mention the fact that I'm expanding a business but I can't go into it now.) Why don't we exchange business cards or phone numbers? I'll give you a call and maybe we can sit down over a coffee. I'd love to run an idea past you."

The direct approach works essentially the same way with a stranger. You use your earlier conversation to identify a "want." You filed it in your head, and at the last minute you selected what you felt to be the best "hot button" for this particular person.

FORM is a wonderful tool, and you should be using it in all conversations as you're out and about meeting people every day. Practice until it becomes natural.

Remember, you can always practice communicating without delivering the (M) message.

Indirect Approach Script

Now it's time to talk about the indirect approach. This is one of my favorites. It doesn't have the same four steps as the direct approach, but I do frequently use step one, which is the introduction. I always use that so that I don't get caught on the telephone too long having to answer questions. Instead, I want to set the appointment.

The indirect approach revolves around location. I use it based on the premise that I'd like to expand my business into the location where the contact happens to live. For example, if I know a certain person lives in Atlanta, Georgia, I might call them and say, "Hi, how are you doing? I've only got a moment, but I've called for a reason. I'm expanding a business in Atlanta, and I thought maybe you might know someone who would like to be in business for themselves. It could mean an extra $5,000 to $7,000 a month for them. "Who do you know?" is an open ended question that requires a name. Never say, "Do you know someone?" It is a closed ended question. It only requires a "yes" or "no" response. Avoid closed ended questions. Stay with "Who do you know?"

Almost without fail they will say, "I might be interested. What's it all about?" At which point, you can give them a little brief overview and set a time to go into more detail either face to face or by telephone. Notice I included an income range. What I try to do is include an income range that is applicable to the particular region of the country in which they are located. For example, if they are in New York or California, I might pick a higher range. If they are in the Midwest, I would keep it lower. I want it to be a good income. I don't want it to be so high it is unbelievable but I also don't want it to be so low that it doesn't get their interest.

I could also use this approach with people I don't know. Have you ever noticed when you're introduced to someone and you say your name, it's not uncommon for them to return with their name and then ask you where you are from? My common statement is, "I'm from Florida, where do you live?" They may say, "I'm from Nashville, Tennessee." When they say where they are from, I touch my head like "You're kidding!" Then I'll proceed to say that I was thinking of expanding a business in Nashville. In fact, you might know someone who may be interested in being in business for themselves. It could mean an extra $3,000 to $5,000 a month. Who do you know?" It's amazing how many times they'll either give you someone's name or they'll say, "Hey, I might be interested."

I've even done the location invitation in reverse. I might begin a conversation by saying "Who do you know in Nashville, Tennessee?" I'm notorious for doing this in an elevator where I have a captive audience. People will look at me like I'm crazy, but invariably someone will ask why. After all, what else do they have to do but look at their feet or the floor display? People rarely look or talk to someone else. If I have four floors, I can usually get the entire invitation out. Let me give you an example:

Paula: "Hi! Who do you know in Nashville?"

Contact: "Why?"

Paula: "I'm expanding my business to Nashville and I'm looking for someone who would be interested in being in business for themselves. It could mean an extra $3,000 to $5,000 a month. Who do you know?

Contact: "I don't know anyone in Nashville. But, would you be interested in expanding your business here in Cincinnati?"

Paula: "Well, I just might. Why don't we exchange numbers and set up a time when we could talk."

Contact: "Great!"

Even if nothing comes of my elevator experiences, I do have fun seeing the reactions of others. I get to make the business a game where everyone wins. In truth, the more you do the unexpected, the more you'll enjoy the reactions and responses of others.

We have so many opportunities to meet people like this and do a location invitation. I know as a new person in the business, sometimes it might be difficult talking to strangers or striking up conversations with people you meet along the way. You don't have to be an expert. You can start small. Keep a tracking list to measure your results. Start by saying "Hi!" Then as you get comfortable, you might be able to say, "Hi, how are you?" It's called scrimmaging, and it can be very good for you. Get comfortable using the **FOR** and don't necessarily deliver the message, or the **M**. Just focus on the **FOR** portion until you become comfortable just talking to people. Eventually you will become more and more comfortable.

In the beginning, though, most of the people you will be inviting to see your business will be people you already know. People whose "hot" buttons you already know will be the easiest place to begin. Later, as you start to get more comfortable with talking to people, you'll be expanding to people you don't know because you're around more people that you don't know than people you know in every day life.

There was a lot of information in this chapter. Look over some of the scripts and practice them. Stop periodically and digest the information. In the next chapter we'll talk about making the presentation. With each step of the process, you are becoming a professional. You're learning a system that is incredibly duplicatable.

CHAPTER 9
Success Is in the Show

Success is not how you do the presentation; it's not where you do the presentation or even how well you do the presentation. Success is the fact that you do it numerous times. **Success is in the show!** If you show the business over and over and over, therein lays your success. In essence, if I had to pick a talent, something that you needed to become really, really good at, it would be the invitation we discussed in the previous chapter. If you could learn a script or a number of scripts and learn to be comfortable inviting people to see the business, you would have a constant flow of people to show. A good invitation leads to many shows.

Be a Winner at the Numbers Game

This is a numbers game where the odds are in your favor. If you practice the principles I'm teaching you in this book, chances are you'll be making money and having a great time doing it. The key is doing it! The more people you show the business to, the greater the chances are that some of those people will join you. It's the same with any kind of marketing out there. If you're in real estate, the more times you show the house, the greater your chances are of selling the house. Network marketing is no different than conventional business in that respect. It is a numbers business.

Why is it we'll accept this in traditional business, but in network marketing we expect everyone who looks at this business to automatically say yes? Perhaps not everyone will see it the way we see it and get involved immediately. Sometimes it takes a number of exposures. Some people may hear good presentations from you and several other network marketers before they'll become involved. Others may never join at all.

For every moment of time you waste being disappointed over someone who fails to get involved with your company, you are losing money, time and momentum. Don't continue to pursue the unattainable—move on. There are plenty of fish in the sea. What's one of the most important words in network marketing? NEXT!

The important thing is to try to do the best presentation you can, showing the biggest picture or vision possible. Don't get hung up on trying to be perfect at the presentation or the circumstances surrounding the presentation. Just show the business. Show it frequently; show it with excitement; show it with enthusiasm; show it with belief. Most importantly, show it with commitment!

Don't Make Yourself the Issue

Focus on the business. When people say yes, they're saying yes to the business. When they say no, they're saying no to the business. Don't take every no personally. Let's say you're on a diet and a Girl Scout shows up at your front door with a box of cookies. If you say, no (heaven forbid you'd say no to a Girl Scout), are you saying no to the Girl Scout or the cookies? It's the cookies, of course. It's the same with network marketing. It is not about you. They are saying no to the business. Just like showing the business, it is not about you. You're the messenger not the message, the delivery agent not the package, the commercial not the show.

When I try to make a point about the message versus the messenger, I frequently use the analogy of Michelin Tire. Let's say Michelin Tire had a tire sale on today: $5 for every tire in stock until they ran out. That would obviously be a pretty good deal. I might buy a couple of tires and store them away until I needed them. If you were a friend of mine, I might call you and say, "Hey, I don't know if you need tires or not, but I just wanted to let you know Michelin has a tire sale today. Five dollars a tire until the stock runs out. I just wanted to let you know."

If you were my friend, would you appreciate my calling to tell you? Sure you would! Do I care whether you buy a tire? Of course not! Do I care whether you know about it? Yes! It's the same way you should feel about your network marketing opportunity. Do you care whether they get involved in the business? No! Do you care whether they know about the business? Yes!

If I was on your list and you waited six months to tell me about the business, I'd be furious. It would definitely affect our friendship. I'd feel that you had wasted six months of precious time for me when I could have been building the business along with you. There are people right now on your list who are friends and associates of yours that you haven't contacted yet. They're not going to be happy when they find out you could have told them about your business six months ago and they could have already been six months into it.

There are people who get into network marketing after seeing the worst presentation. There are people who don't get in after seeing the best presentation. They either see it or they don't. Give the best message you can give. Give it your best shot. Be the best you can be. You don't have to try to be someone else. You don't have to be perfect or an expert. Just tell your story and be yourself. Either they will see it or they won't.

It was liberating for me to realize that it wasn't me. I felt so relieved. My whole attitude changed. The process and numbers became the issue, not me. When you get on the phone, don't apologize. Don't say, "Please, if you could only give me thirty minutes of your time. Maybe I could show it to you in twenty minutes. In fact, I could probably do it in fifteen minutes. Please, please, please!" Remember, you're not the issue. Be dignified. You are the sorter, you have the right to choose. There is no need to sell, convince or plead.

How Do I Show? Let Me Count the Ways!

I am going to cover all the various ways the business can be shown. Because of the growth of new technologies our choices continue to grow, however many people are still building a business face-to-face. I don't want to leave any option out. I have used them all.

With the use of tools available, anyone can present this business. Many companies will have conference calls, on-line opportunity presentations, DVDs as well as CDs for you to give to contacts. As long as your contact can push play, they can hear about your business. These are also great tools for you to learn and memorize the presentation.

At the same time, many companies will have local business briefings or company opportunity presentations that you can attend with your guest. It is important, though, that you try to learn the presentation as soon as possible so that you can have the freedom to show it any time, any place, all by yourself. We have a saying: "The person that holds the marker makes the money!"

One of the best ways to learn the presentation is to immediately record a presentation of one or several people in the business that you aspire to be like. If there is a presentation going on in your area, at a hotel or a local meeting room or even on a conference call, you need to tape it. Then, transcribe it, memorize every aspect of the presentation until it becomes yours, and recite it verbatim for your presentations. You can even transcribe a CD and learn it until it is you.

Different Strokes for Different Folks:

The One on One Presentation

Let's talk for a few moments about the different kinds of presentations. The first kind is a face-to-face presentation with one or two people. We call them one-on-ones. You can even invite your sponsor or someone else in your upline to help. It can be held at a home, an office or even a restaurant. There are really no restrictions as to where this kind of a presentation can take place. It's important that you have materials with you about your company. The more documentation you have to add to the company's credibility, the better. Also, you might want to have some sample products—definitely some pictures of products as well so they can see how professional the literature and product are with this particular company.

The Small Group Presentation

A second kind of presentation is with small groups. This type of presentation could be held at a boardroom, a home or an office, any place where you can fit in a number of people to hear the presentation. You can either do the presentation or you can have your upline help you do the presentation.

The Large Group Presentation

The third type of meeting is a large group presentation. This is usually held at a hotel or a large meeting room. Large meetings are nice because there are a number of people in attendance who usually do testimonials to add to the documentation and credibility of the company. It also adds to the enthusiasm of the meeting so that your guest can see that many people are excited about this particular company. This is a way of endorsing your product and company.

The Conference Call Presentation

In today's world where people are putting in long hours at work and trying to juggle family and career, time is a very precious commodity. I believe this is why conference calling has become one of the most popular methods of showing and building a business. Now we can just invite someone to listen in on a call and virtually hear much of the content and enthusiasm that they hear if they were at a large meeting.

It's usually a fifteen to twenty minute phone presentation where you can have a guest call a designated number and listen to a presentation of the business. It is also very common for the speaker to have others on the line giving testimonials as to their experience with the company or validating the effectiveness of the product.

Presentation Format

Showing the presentation in network marketing is easy. You can use a CD/DVD and website or if a live meeting is available, you can attend and even learn the presentation for yourself so that you can have the freedom to show it anywhere, any time, any place. Like almost everything else in network marketing, you should do the presentation like those who are successful. Hopefully they make it duplicatable.

I always had a certain outline in my head that I followed. During the presentation, I'd first begin talking about the trends that lead up to my particular company and why this company would fit right into today's consumer needs and desires. I would discuss the current high demand for my company's product or service. I would give an overview of the company itself. Next, I would cover information about the various products we had to offer. I would also talk about the compensation plan and the income opportunity. I would explain the training and support that's available in my organization and with my company. Finally, I would share the rewards and recognition people receive by joining our team of network marketers.

That was the outline. If the guest interrupted with a question, I would still know what the outline was and I could always pick up where I left off. I wouldn't have to start all over from the beginning.

There are also some people who have created what we call "pitch books," which are a very duplicatable method of showing the business. These are books that have the presentation, usually in PowerPoint, in a convenient, easy to carry binder. They go through the book showing the presentation. A person can use a pitch book quite effectively if they pull it out as a last minute idea so it doesn't seem so canned. "By the way, I do have some literature here and maybe I can pull this out for you to look through as I'm explaining this opportunity." Otherwise, if you don't have a pitch book you certainly want to have some brochures and literature so you can show the professionalism of your company. Show it on a tablet of paper if you need to draw things out or have it already drawn out in order to point to things as you present. Remember, people learn differently—some learn by hearing, some by seeing.

Focus on the "Why" Not the "How"

What's important when you're showing the presentation is that you stay focused on the "why." Don't get into the "how." You have to understand that when people see a presentation for the first time, they are looking for two things: 1) the catch, and 2) the reason that you want to share it with them. It's the old "What's in it for you" suspicion. After all, in the traditional world no one gives a golden opportunity away. No one finds a way to help someone else afford a new home, new car, quit their present job or change their life by becoming financially independent. It just doesn't happen.

Consequently, if you spend too much time getting into the "how," it'll leave the door open for people looking for catches or reasons why not to do it, or read into things and create reasons that don't exist.

I remember one presentation that had to do with water filters. The company had a large home unit and the presenter said the home unit needed to be installed by a plumber. Now that was a very innocent statement, but that statement was a "how" statement, not a "why" statement. You want to focus on why people should do the business and why it can change their lives, not all the specifics on how to do it. With that one little statement, even though it was innocent, here is what could happen when a couple drives home after seeing the presentation. They are very excited about the business at first. Then, all of a sudden they start questioning what that presenter meant by needing a plumber to install that particular water unit. The conversation might have sounded like this:

"Does that mean we need to become plumbers?"

"Do we need to go to plumbing school?"

"How much do you think it will cost to go to plumbing school?"

"I don't know, but I'm sure it's more than we want to pay."

"What will our friends think if we become plumbers?"

"Maybe the presenter meant that we needed to hire a plumber to work for us."

"How much do you think the going rate for a plumber is these days?"

"I'm sure that most of them are union; it must be very expensive."

"Oh, I don't think we can do this business. In fact, when the person that invited us calls back, you just tell them that we don't have time. Tell them we're not interested because we don't have time."

In this case, the person who invited them would never know the real reason these people decided not to get in the business. It was all because of an innocent "how" statement during a presentation when the distributor should have been focused on the "why."

Understand Other People's Fears

When people look at an opportunity presentation, they bring with them a number of fears. For example, they bring with them the fear of whether this company will work, the fear of failure, the fear of what their friends will think, the fear of wondering whether they have to quit their jobs and put their family at risk, the fear of how much money they will have to invest into the business, and perhaps even the fear of going through the family savings before they are able to see a profit.

What I try to do is to keep all their fears in mind so that I can share with them during the presentation certain things that will eliminate their fears. For example, I will spend a great deal of time on the credibility of the company so they will not only feel comfortable that this company is financially strong, but, at the same time, they'll feel proud to tell people what they know about the company. I'll also mention that many people start part-time so they know they would not have to quit their jobs and put their families and their finances at risk. I also talk about how seriously they need to treat the business. I explain to them that if they treat it like a hobby it will pay like a hobby. That's why, if they're serious, they need to start the business by giving it every waking moment they have outside of their jobs. I'll talk about the possibilities of beginning this business with minimal start-up costs: basic product, basic literature. We're not talking about a major franchise operation. They can begin at a reasonable starting point and build from there.

Most companies will have a buy back policy. This is one thing I recommend you check on when looking at a company. In most cases, starting with a network company is really no financial risk for anyone. The only risk is maybe a little loss of time. But rewards can be huge if you're willing to take that risk!

Another fear on the part of the guest might be the fear of not knowing what to do and not having much help during the learning process. It's really the fear of failure. Looking at it from their perspective, network marketing is a whole new way of doing business for them. Even in traditional business they don't always get the proper help and training. They may have worked for new companies that offered very little training or support. So they had to learn everything the hard way, and that means a lot of pressure on them and their families. When people express this fear, I talk about the help and support that's supplied and all the tools, materials and technology that the company has provided to help them be successful. I make it clear to them that they have an entire upline that has a vested interest in their success. In fact, their upline doesn't make money until they make money first. So, it is to their upline's advantage to help them succeed because that's the only way the upline succeeds.

Control the Distractions During the Presentation

It is most important to control the distractions during the presentation, whether it is a one-on-one, a small group, large group or a conference call. It's up to you to control the distractions. The minute someone's distracted, you have to pull them back into the presentation. If they are distracted at a large presentation they may miss just enough of the presentation to be lost from that point on. During a one-on-one presentation, you can control the distractions by making sure you are meeting in a place where you won't be disturbed. In a small group presentation, say at a home, it's important that you try to control the distractions such as the telephone, pets and/or children. If you are meeting at a home, preferably, it will be your home; it's easier to control things there.

If you are doing a presentation in a home with a small group, ask the host to take the phone off the hook. Make sure all pets are secured some place. Make sure the children are being watched by a babysitter, or perhaps in bed. In a large group presentation, it's important that you and your guest don't get up and leave the meeting during the presentation. If your guest has a question, ask them to remember it and you will answer it at the end. As a courtesy for everyone else's guest, control distractions as best you can.

Make a Good First Impression

How you dress for a presentation will vary depending on the circumstances. There are many different opinions on this particular topic, but let me share with you my thoughts. During a one-on-one presentation, I attempt to dress in the same way I expect the contact to be dressed. For example, if the meeting was on a Saturday in their home and I expected them to be in casual attire, I would not wear a business suit. I would wear casual attire. By casual I don't mean dirty blue jeans and a ragged t-shirt. I would dress nicely, neatly, but casual. If I'm doing a small presentation with a group of people that I've never met, then I would be dressed in business attire. I would make sure that the host knows that I'll be dressed in a suit. If it's a business presentation at a hotel, I would definitely be dressed in a business suit. It's important that you never let your guest out dress you at any meeting, whether it's a hotel meeting or a home meeting.

One of the reasons that you always dress in business attire at a hotel meeting is because you want people to feel comfortable to invite their bank president or a top professional that they know. The entire atmosphere should be very professional. You wouldn't want to invite a top caliber professional to a presentation and have people in blue jeans and tennis shoes, would you? It would be difficult for your guest to take the business seriously. People will make forty decisions about you during that first meeting. It's your opportunity to make every one of them a positive one. Make sure that first impression delivers the message you want delivered. As the old saying goes "You only have one chance to make a good first impression."

Meeting Setup

Now let's talk about presentation setup and etiquette. These things are more important for groups.

Small Group Presentation Setup

If the small group meeting is in the home, do not rearrange the furniture. Add chairs or move chairs as necessary when people arrive. When you confirm appointments to see just how much room and how many chairs you'll need, call the person the night before and say, "Hi, this is so and so. Did I tell you 7:00 tomorrow night or 7:30?" They will say, "You said 7:30." You'll respond with "Great, just wanted to check. See you then." This way you'll be confirming the time and reminding them about that presentation.

If the presentation is not at your home it is a good idea if you can chauffer your guest to the meeting. Then you will always be sure they will be in attendance. If that's not possible, it's important that you try to confirm. Don't be surprised if not everyone shows up for the presentation. That was probably the most disappointing part for me when I first started network marketing. I would invite ten people to a presentation and maybe only two or three would actually show. I really took it personally at first. It's important that you don't do that. You need to understand that you're going to learn a lot about people as you start to build a network marketing business, and those people that you thought were reliable and dependable may turn out to be just the opposite. What's important for you is to focus on the people who do show and not the ones who don't.

During a home presentation, I try not to have any kind of flip chart or white board set out. If I need one, I will pull it out once I've done an introduction and gotten started with the presentation. I will make sure my props are close by. In fact during my initial welcome, I might say, "Hi! This is what we're going to talk about. In fact, it would be helpful if I had a prop here that I could write on." At this point I'd pull it out. That way, no one has a preconceived idea of how the presentation will proceed or how it compares to another presentation or meeting.

One of the things I'll mention at the beginning of the presentation is for the guests to save all their questions until the end. I explain to them that they'll find most of their questions answered throughout the presentation. By doing this, you'll be less distracted, and you can control what could appear to be a negative question in a less threatening one-on-one situation.

At the end of the presentation, it's good for the presenter to say, "Why don't we take a break for some refreshments. This will give you a chance to look at some of the literature and see some of the products that our company markets." Then the host will get up and everyone will get up and stretch. People will naturally begin to separate. Then I have a chance to go to the one person who I thought might have had a skeptical look and deal with their questions privately. At the same time any other distributors in the room, or the host, can answer specific questions on a one-to-one basis. If someone has a concern that really doesn't apply to everyone, it can be addressed privately. In the meantime, refreshments are kept very simple, maybe coffee, lemonade or iced tea to drink in Styrofoam cups. If there is anything to eat, make it store-bought cookies served on paper plates with napkins. Remember the KISS principle: Keep it simple sweetheart! Make sure everything you do is duplicatable. That way a guest won't think "I can't get in this business because if we have a presentation in our home, we'll have to serve baked Alaska on good china." You want to keep the business very simple and very duplicatable. Paper plates, cups, coffee and store-bought cookies is very duplicatable.

The Large Group Setup

For a larger meeting at a hotel, here are a few extra tips. First, it's important that the temperature of the room be cool. Cool air keeps people alert. I would also advise that the lights be turned up as bright as they can be to keep people awake. You never set up more chairs than the number of people you expect. It's better to have them stacked in the back of the room and pull them out, as you need them rather than for it to appear as though you expected a hundred people and only thirty showed.

Have some upbeat music playing when people enter the room so it's an uplifting atmosphere. At a hotel or large presentation, you want to have a very professional product display as well as a board to write on or a screen to show a PowerPoint presentation. If necessary, lights can be slightly dimmed. This way the audience can see you and you can still be interacting with the audience. Keep in mind this is all personal preference. I usually use a laptop computer and LCD/DLP projector. You may feel differently about presentation materials. Experiment! It's your business. You're in control!

At the end of the presentation with a large group in a hotel room, it's nice to be able to arrange your chairs in a little circle to be able to talk to your guests and answer their questions. This creates a more intimate, private atmosphere. It's always important to introduce your line of sponsorship and edify them so your guest will respect what they say. Your upline can add credibility to you and show the guest that you have quite a line of support to help when needed. They can also endorse the business and edify you. One of the strengths of your program might just be the testimony of what the business has done for your sponsor. Hopefully, the presentation already had a few testimonials at the end that documented and endorsed the product and the company. It's always nice to have a one-on-one testimonial right there to make it more believable.

It is extremely helpful if you can introduce your guest to someone already in the business that has something in common with your guest, like the same occupation.

About Those Testimonials

While on the topic of testimonials, I would like to say a few words on how a proper testimonial should be given. First, let's talk about the importance of testimonials. Testimonials are more important than the actual presentation. They really endorse the company, product and you. Done correctly, testimonials can make a presentation—done wrong they can ruin the presentation. Most testimonials are done at the end of the business presentation, and that is when the presenter will actually invite a few people to talk of their experiences with the product and/or business. These are usually people from the audience.

The strongest testimonials are the ones that come from the audience, and are selected ahead of time. When a guest is sitting in the audience, they do not know if the person giving the testimonial is a distributor or another guest like themselves. Consequently, when that person stands up, whether they make the testimonial from their seat or come up front, they still remain a part of the audience. It's important that they maintain that posture. Let me tell you what I mean. The presenter is the person who the guests are least likely to believe, or whom they are most likely to be skeptical of because the presenter is really selling you on the company. When those giving testimonials come up to the front, they are still part of the audience. They are still believable. The minute they start selling the company, they become the presenter — unbelievable.

How do you keep a testimonial believable? You keep it simple. Keep the person from pitching the company. Here's an example of a testimonial broken down into four steps. Share this with your downline before they have the occasion to give a testimonial.

1. They give their name/location is optional
2. Their present or past occupation
3. What attracted them to this company
4. What has happened or what they hope will happen

For example, "My name is John Smith. I am currently an accountant. I got involved in this business so that my wife could quit her job. She wants to stay home full-time to raise our children. As of today we're halfway there." Or "My name is Susan Daily. I am an attorney. My goal was to be able to leave my practice, be totally free so I could travel and become a wildlife photographer. I want to be self-employed. I just turned in my two weeks notice and will be full-time as of next month."

What to Avoid in Testimonials

What you really don't want the person giving the testimonial to say is "This is the greatest company since sliced bread. You need to get involved. Come join us. We're having a great time." That is selling the business. All of a sudden he has changed from being seen as a member of the audience to a presenter/salesman. Now he becomes unbelievable as well. A testimonial should go no more than thirty seconds. It should make a point. It should sizzle!

In the case of a product testimony, simply give your name, your present or past occupation, what attracted you to the product and what's happened so far. You may want to elaborate a little bit on what the results have been since you have been using the product. Throw in a few enthusiastic adjectives and you have a dynamite testimony.

Even in the Testimonials—Be Duplicatable

I can't emphasize this enough—in everything you do, be duplicatable. The more you elaborate, the more the next person will feel they need to. The next thing you know, your testimonials are going five to ten minutes long. It's like gaining weight.

Even your steps in a testimonial need to be duplicatable. Anyone can talk about those four things. If you start adding other steps to it, you've got to make sure that the answers you're going to get are going to be things you want an audience to hear. For instance, if you want them to say how they got started, not everyone will have gotten started the same way. So, if you want a person to get started right, and you have the testimonial of someone who started right, that's good. If the next testimonial is someone who didn't start right, that's not so good. It's not a duplicatable addition to your testimonials unless you can control it.

Proper Meeting Attitude

As a part of the audience it's important that you smile and show energy and excitement. Act like you're really interested in whatever is being said. That "meeting attitude" will radiate to other people in the audience. There is a saying that the speaker is only as good as the audience, and I know, first hand, the truth of that statement. When I am the speaker, I know that the distributors in that audience who have brought a guest want me to do well.

In order for me to do the best for them, they need to do the best for me. The best for me would be to see their smiles, hear their laughter at my jokes (no matter how many times they have heard them) and to see interested eyes (no sleepy, half closed lids). Be as excited to hear the presenter the fiftieth time you've heard that same presentation as you were the first, and your guests will sense your enthusiasm and match your emotion. Remember: a speaker is only as good as his or her audience.

The Presentation After the Presentation

I'm a big believer in taking fifteen minutes after a presentation to go through what I refer to as a **Fast Start**. The reason I like doing these after group presentations, either with a small or large group, is because I can control some of the words that are used. I can keep it very general and not get into specific "hows." I can also eliminate some of the fears of the guests. I have already discussed the fears a person might have when they first look at the business. A Fast Start can answer those fears and other questions buried in the guest's mind. If the person who invited them to the presentation is a novice, it will certainly supply the answers they are too new to have.

Five Step Fast Start Program

This program will take away some of the fears and help answer the questions that a new distributor may be having difficulty addressing with their guests. I'm really helping that new distributor learn more about the business, and I'm helping the distributor answer the questions for their guests. The Fast Start has five components:

1. Determine what you (the guest) want
2. Educate yourself
3. Start right
4. Develop a business
5. Educate others

Before I get started on the Fast Start, we usually take a short fifteen-minute break after the presentation so people can get up, stretch, go the restroom, get some refreshments and mingle a bit. If I tell them that after the short break we're going to show them in fifteen minutes how to build the business, they'll probably stay. If I say 20 - 30 minutes, they may not want to stay. Remember, when you tell them fifteen minutes, you better have them out of there in that time frame.

Keep in mind a Fast Start is not a presentation a new distributor should be doing. This is something that you'll want to add to your presentation.

Step 1: Determine What You Want

The goal is to help the guest determine what they want out of this business. Communicate to them that all their dreams can become a reality if they work hard enough. I want them to understand they need to treat this business seriously. I also let them know that they don't have to quit their jobs to begin building their business. I let them know that if they give it every waking moment around their present job, they can get their income to match what they are presently making on their job. Then they can decide if they want to go full-time, or would prefer to continue along the same path. At this time, I make it clear that there are people making an extra five hundred dollars a month in the business, as well as people making five or six figure incomes per month.

What I really want to do is to help them understand that this is not just a cute, little part-time endeavor. This is a serious business that could give them serious income and totally change their lives. I want them to understand, from day one, they need to determine what they want and based on what they want, develop a plan of action that will help them get it. If someone wants to make an extra thousand dollars a month, I'll help them do that. If somebody else wants to make ten thousand a month, we'll set up a different plan specifically for them. Most importantly, they have to communicate their expectations, needs and dreams to their upline in order to put together the appropriate plan of action.

Step 2: Educate Yourself

The goal of this section is to review the tools available to a new distributor to learn the business. Discuss the starter kit, websites, literature, brochures, CDs and DVDs available to them. If applicable, tell them about conference calls, training sessions and events that the company provides. Explain there is a line of sponsorship available to help them, as well as their own sponsor to help them step-by-step. All of this assures the guest that they will not be left alone. Let them know that even the top producers went through the same process they are going through right now. But they trusted the process, the company and the support system.

Step 3: Start Right

Next discuss how important it is to get off to the right start. I use analogies because I want to compare this to things they understand, things in traditional businesses. I might say to them, "Would it make sense if you're getting involved with a company that you would want to get familiar with the product? The best way to get familiar would be to use it, wouldn't you agree? How could you speak about all its benefits if you had not experienced them first hand?" Then I talk to them about inventory. "Would it make sense if you were in any other kind of business that you would probably have at least one of everything?" They shake their heads yes. Then I use a McDonald's analogy. "What do you think would happen if you spent the money for a McDonald's franchise only to inform McDonald's you would be interested in carrying the Big Mac, the Quarter Pounder, the fries, but they could keep the fish fillet because you hate fish? They'd say, "You're out of here!" Why? Because they know their business, and they would know you wouldn't be successful.

What I'm trying to get across to the audience is that this is a business, not a pick and choose menu. They should become as familiar as they can with everything the company has to offer. It doesn't mean that they need to be an expert. It just means that they are going to want to start with some product. I do make it clear, however, that the company doesn't require that they purchase anything. I appeal to their logic, their common sense.

I also explain that this is not a door-to-door business. Our product is marketed through interactive marketing, not through event sales. Event sales are when you set an appointment. It becomes an event. You go to an office or home to present something. You lay out your materials or your pitch book or whatever, and it's a sales event. Not everyone can do that.

That is not how network marketing works. We don't go door-to-door. This really relaxes the audience a little bit because that's one of their greatest fears. I talk about interactive selling. Our business, our product is marketed through interaction. In other words, we use it, we like it, people ask us about it — we tell them our story and invite them to use it themselves. We do interactive selling every day of our lives; we just don't get paid for it. If you've ever told someone about a great movie you saw or an excellent restaurant you've been to — guess what? You just became their network marketer, only you didn't get paid for the fine job you did of spreading the word. Theaters, restaurants, doctors, attorneys, accountants and many other professionals depend on word of mouth for a great deal of their business, only they call it referral business. Same thing—network marketing is about using a product, liking it and when you are asked by another about it, telling your story and pretty soon those who hear your story buy your product and may get involved in your business as well. Interactive marketing at its best!

Step 4: Develop a Business

I cover this briefly since I am trying to stay within fifteen minutes. This is where I share my Coca Cola analogy that was presented earlier.

Using the Coca Cola analogy, I develop an understanding of opportunity and timing, and I ask them to think about just how easy it is to overlook now what could be worth a fortune down the road. I remind the audience they should consider it an honor to be introduced to and to introduce others to this business and they should recognize the urgency of taking advantage of this opportunity. We are looking for partners and associates. We are looking for runners — people who want to run with us side-by-side.

Step 5: Educate Others

Explain that what we learn, we teach. We help our new distributors do the same thing we're doing. It's a cycle. In fact, I show a diagram that shows how it comes full circle. They decide what they want, they get educated, they start right; they learn the techniques of building a business, then they educate others on the same things.

Conclusion

Just to review: new distributors will determine what they want, educate themselves, start right, develop their business and then educate others to determine what they want, educate themselves and so on.

If a new distributor learns and practices the five steps really well, it can lead to financial success. The business is really not complicated. It is learning five simple things very well and simply teaching those five steps to the people who join them in their business.

Helping Your Guest Make the Decision

How do you help that new guest make a decision, and then how do you follow-up? You know, it's amazing how many of us want our new guest to make a decision to get involved right on the spot, yet when we look at ourselves, most of us didn't make a decision the first time we saw the business. Most of us made a decision after receiving more information, seeing it a few times, getting all our questions answered and so on.

Don't have unrealistic expectations of your guests. Do some guests make decisions the first time they see it? You bet! In fact, Napoleon Hill once said "Successful people make decisions quickly and are slow to change their minds while unsuccessful people make decisions slowly and are quick to change their minds." It's not unusual for a person very focused and on purpose to make a decision immediately, but it's also important that there is a process involved here. There's a process in getting people to see the business. There's a process in getting them to finally make a decision. As long as we have a number of people in that process, we have people making decisions every day because they're moving to that decision point.

At the end of the presentation, DON'T BE AFRAID TO ASK! One of the biggest mistakes people make is that they never ask their guest if they want to get involved in the business. Instead of asking for a decision, they'll say, "Would you like to take some literature home with you?" Now, if this person is ready to get involved in the business and you ask them that question, they are naturally going to say, "Yes, of course." Then if you call them in a couple of days to ask them if they would like to see a DVD or listen to a CD, they're going to say "Yes, of course." Then you eventually invite them to listen to a conference call and during the call there is the mention of a starter kit, they say to you, "Where's my starter kit?" Don't be so quick to congratulate yourself. You just cost them two weeks of actively working the business because you didn't ask them for a decision in the very beginning. Wasting two weeks of their time may not be something for which they thank you. Plus what are you teaching them, by example, to duplicate?

By the way, I don't believe in having anyone at a training session that is not a distributor. A guest has no place listening to a training class. All it will do is feed their skeptical reasoning as why **not** to do the business. Training mostly focuses on the **how**.

Learning how to ask questions is an important part of this business. You need to know when, where, how and why to ask questions. That's what we'll be learning in the next chapter. Don't expect perfect little canned questions to go with a perfect little canned presentation. Instead of learning the exact questions, you'll learn about types and styles of questions to ask. You'll learn when and how to ask them. When you've learned that, you can make them your own and others will enjoy the natural, easy manner in which you present this business. Most important, when you are comfortable, you teach others to be the same. They duplicate your performance, and soon you have an organization of great presenters.

CHAPTER 10

A Time for Questions— A Time to Act

It's just as important to know when and how to ask questions as it is to know the types of questions to ask. Some questions are better asked when inviting while others bring better results when asked toward the end of the presentation. Since we have already covered some of our questioning techniques when we discussed scripting the invitation, we'll now talk about questions that follow the presentation. There are three questions that I have used quite successfully at the end of a presentation. They are:

1. What did they like best? (It's amazing how many times they'll say, "The money!")

2. Where do you see yourself? (They'll usually say "At the top!")

3. When would you like to receive your first check? (A frequent answer is "Yesterday!")

Note that all three questions at the end of the presentation were open-ended questions as covered earlier. By asking them open-ended questions like the three above, you are asking the contact to think and actually respond with more than a one-word answer. You are leading the conversation. It moves as you direct it. You are in control but the atmosphere is low-pressure and easy.

Let's say you have a new distributor ready to get started in the business with you. Now what do you do to help them? My best advice is to do with them what your sponsor did with you. Hopefully, he or she took you through the getting started stages as outlined in this book. If you were smart, you recorded everything you were told so you could memorize, transcribe and learn that information for yourself. If so, you can now do the same with your new person.

Another great question is, "What more information do you need to make a decision"? This is my favorite and usually leads to a faster conclusion since I know what it is going to take.

Teach by Example

Do everything the same way each time so your new distributors can learn quickly and teach the same to their new distributors. It's important that you do everything exactly the way it was done for you. Why would you want to deviate from what has made your sponsor and upline successful in the business.

When you set up a business planning session, your people should be taping what you do. You in turn should be doing exactly what was done with you. Have we gone over duplication enough, now? Believe it or not, there will be some who will still persist in doing everything their own way and stretching out that learning curve. This only leads to maximum frustration on their part and those in their downline. It's just not fair to do that to yourself or to those in your organization. Hopefully, with an active line of sponsorship, the proper message will get across many times to eliminate delays.

If you're new, your upline should sit down with you and your new distributor, in person or over the phone, to help do a business planning session. Doing it together gives you the opportunity to hear it again and get it down properly. Your upline should help you with two or three planning sessions, so by the time you have seen the same session over and over, you should be able to do the next one proficiently by youself. That's why it is so important at the initial business presentation to introduce your line of sponsorship. In a face to face presentation this is easy. If you are not face to face, simply do a three-way call with your upline. By introducing your upline, it gives them power to also influence your new person in a positive way.

Involving your upline helps in two ways. One, it shows that new guest or new person that there's going to be more than just you helping them. This gives them some security. Secondly it gives you the advantage of having your guests hear someone else endorse the business and you.

It sometimes helps your new distributor to hear another voice. It's amazing how they can hear the same message from a different person and they'll pick up things they didn't hear when you said it the first time. If your upline is saying the same things you have said, eventually the message is going to sink in.

Keep in mind your introduction adds credibility to your line of sponsorship so your new recruit will think they need to listen to what is being said. Also, your line of sponsorship should say great things about you so your new person feels fortunate to have you as a sponsor. In network marketing we call this mutual respect: edification.

Edify Your Upline

I give my upline the power by introducing and complimenting them to my new guest, giving them credibility and the power to step in and help me when necessary. By edifying my upline I keep their name in my guest's mind. If my guest doesn't relate to me, maybe one of the upline sponsors will strike a rapport and help get him or her involved. It works both ways. When my upline comes to meet my new guest, they should edify me in return. They should say, "Boy, you couldn't have picked a better person to help you with the business should you decide to get involved!"

What Objections Should You Expect?

Network marketing is a $100 billion business worldwide. You rarely hear the kind of objections against network marketing you may have heard years ago. It is an accepted business strategy today and those involved have well-known success stories. If our system is to be duplicatable, it has to be simple so that anyone can do it—including answering any objections. One of the methods I was taught early in my network marketing career was the FEEL, FELT, FOUND concept.

I Feel, Felt, Found My Way Through Almost Every Objection

How do you respond when someone has an objection? I could give you elaborate responses designed to answer every objection in great detail. I could have devoted page after page of this book to answering almost every possible objection you could ever hear, Lord knows I've probably heard them all. The only problem with that is you'd have to be a world-class weight lifter to pick up the book. And memorizing pages of responses is not duplicatable. I'd rather stick with the KISS method and use the simple feel, felt, found method to answer objections. Here's how it works.

Let's suppose someone has an objection such as: "I bet you have to have a sales background to do this." Rather than starting a circular argument by saying, "No you don't," and them saying "I bet you do," use the **feel, felt, found** method. Simply say I know how you **feel. I felt** the same way. I thought you needed a sales background. Then I found you didn't need that at all. In fact, let me introduce you to so and so who is a mechanic. Or, let me introduce you to this person over here who's a teacher." It's wonderful if you can use examples of others. If someone says "Well, I think I'm too young or too old" simply say, "I know how you **feel. I felt** the same way, and then I **found** that you didn't have to be that concerned about age. In fact, let me point out so and so who has been retired twenty years and is just starting this business." Can you see how this would set their minds to rest? And the feel, felt found method can be used with almost any objection.

Try it, you'll like it. It is very disarming! It is one of the most natural ways to answer objections you'll ever experience, and really quite duplicatable. For example, the old "I don't have the time" objection can be answered with "Boy, I know how you feel. I felt the same way. I was really busy, and then I found that I could build this around my job. With some effort, I could match the income I was making on my present job." Or, if the objection is "I bet you need a lot of money to get started," you might say, "I know how you feel. I felt the same way, and then I found out that the initial start-up costs were very minimal." Practice! I have yet to find an objection that feel, felt, found can't address.

Don't Take the Objections or "Nos" Personally

I've said it before, but I'm going to say it again. You can't afford to take the "nos" in this business personally. I've seen people lose a month's momentum over one or two little "no" responses. Think about it! I have seen people turn a three second disappointment into three weeks. Doesn't make much sense, does it? When this happens, people start saying to themselves, "I don't know if this business is going to work for me."

I'm there to give my distributors all the support they need but when someone starts questioning their abilities or the business just because someone said no, you know what I say? "GET OVER IT!" Okay, it sounds like I don't care but, in reality, it is because I do care that I can say this. Believe me, when you are feeling that sorry for yourself, you don't need another person crying with you. You need someone to be tough and send you back out there to collect the "yes" waiting for you. It is always the case. Times seem their bleakest just before you are going to hit pay dirt.

Remember, this is a numbers game. Understand the ratios but know it's not always predictable. The first fifteen people to whom you show the product or business might say "no" and the following five might say "yes." After you show a significant number of people, the ratios will be there. Let's go over those numbers one more time. On average, using warm market or referrals, out of five people you show the business to, one will get involved (initially your numbers will be worse). That means that for every five people who get involved, one will actually do something. Don't kid yourself! There will be people who get involved with the business who don't do anything. Eventually, after you become experienced, your ratios should be around one in three. That means, for every three people who get involved, one will do something. Of the three who get involved, one should build a good business, one should build a small business and one will do absolutely nothing. The key reason that someone fails in this business is that they spend the majority of their time with people who will never make a dime.

I believe in the buoyancy of leadership. What do I mean by that? Well, the leaders will rise to the top! They'll be the ones who will be calling you, asking for help. Those are the ones with whom you need to spend the majority of your time. Remember this: you are not responsible for everyone's success!

If your ratio is one in five, then that means you show five people to sponsor one. You need about five people in your business to have one that's going to do something. If you need five people who are going to do something, and your ratio is one to five, you're probably going to have to sponsor twenty-five to have five serious people.

Do you see why I am always saying **the key to success is in the show?** It's not in the sign because there will be people who sign up in this business and do nothing. In fact, there will be people who sign up in the business, buy product and do nothing. That's the most amazing part. Network marketing is no different than the numbers of traditional business, so accept the numbers. Determine what your ratios are, then go for it.

Remember my Coca Cola analogy. You're not out to coax or convince. You're looking to identify the people who are going to run with you, side-by-side, and share in the fortunes to be made through network marketing. Success is in the show. That is the only thing that you can control. How many times do you show the business? If you're going to be an expert, be an expert at the invitation. That way you have plenty of people to show. The key to your success is in the show, show, show, show, show! If someone says, "yes" you say "great!" If someone says, "no!" you say "great!" Just show, show, show, show —NEXT—show, show, and show some more!

Think of It As the Job Interview

When I say success is in the show, I also mean it is not in the sell. Don't ever sell somebody on this business. Have you ever been to a job interview? If it was a job you really wanted, let's say with a very successful company, a fortune 500 company, you were probably pretty excited! For the interview, you would probably dress professionally and even practice in your mind some of the answers to the questions you think they might ask. You would expect the interviewer to be calm and in control of the interview, wouldn't you? After all, they're not the one worrying. They already have a job with this dream company!

What you would try to do is make a good impression and have all the right answers. Now let me ask you a question. What if halfway through the interview, the interviewer climbed over the table, grabbed you by the jacket and said, "Please, please, please, take this job!" What would you think? Wouldn't you think something was desperately wrong with the company? The fact that they were begging you to take the job would be a strong indication that there was something wrong! You would be concerned that anything you had heard previously about the company was inaccurate. If you thought they were successful, you'd now believe that maybe they were in trouble and that's why they needed you. Sometimes we do this exact same thing in network marketing. We may not be as blatant, but we still do it. Let me set the scene:

A distributor is showing guests the business. He shows them all the statistics and credentials verifying the company's reputation. He tells them how great the company is, how wonderful the product is and how profitable the compensation program is. He shows them all the potential of the opportunity. AND THEN… he leans forward and tries to sell them and convince them to get into the business. The more they lean back, the more he leans forward. When he does that, here is the message he is delivering: "Please, please, please join my organization. I'm desperate!" The guest begins to think, "Why do they need me so badly? The company must be in trouble. If it were so great, why would they need to beg me to join?" He has just canceled out all the company's credibility!

If he believed this opportunity was similar to Coca Cola, he would be comfortably leaning back in that chair, and the guests would be leaning forward to catch his every word. He wouldn't be selling them. They'd be selling him on why he should pick them. He would be sitting up straight, confident that he had a great opportunity to offer, and they would feel lucky he had chosen them as a partner or associate. After all, he has the right to choose who he wants to work with as an associate.

I don't mean that arrogantly; I mean that confidently. There is a difference. So, keep your posture. You need to come from a point of strength. You are looking for people with the same vision who want to run with you. Unfortunately, those people are going to be few and far between, so you need to be patient. Once you find them, you'll never go back to trying to coax and convince anyone again. Once you find somebody with the same vision, you'll know exactly what you're looking for and you won't settle for less.

Your Group Should Motivate You

Do you remember my personal story of how I began in this business? I shared with you the story of working for fifteen months and realizing that my group didn't excite me. It just didn't motivate me! I hope you learned something from that shared experience. Your group should excite you. It should motivate you through the members' enthusiasm and actions. If not, you've got the wrong group.

Sometimes you have to start over. Most people who have made it to the top have started over, sometimes more than once. They've had some people on board, but they weren't the right people and they had to start over to get people who motivated them. From the very beginning, if you understand the numbers and work them consistently, your chances for success are excellent.

If you have to start over and recruit different people, your organization will be better because of it. You will be better also, because you will have learned something in the process. You'll have a different attitude. You will have learned to come from a position of strength. No more dilly-dallying around with the people who are acting like they want to be successful but aren't willing to do the work it takes.

What Will Bring Me Financial Success?

In this chapter, I've saved the best for last—money! What are the money-making activities in network marketing? If I simplify this business and break it down to the key activities that make you money, there are just two: showing the product and showing the business. Those are the only ways you truly make money in network marketing. Just like a retail store, it's important for you to cash out at the end of every day. Ask yourself how many times you showed the business. How many times did you show the product? If you didn't do either one, you didn't make any money. You constantly need to be reminding yourself of that, especially in the beginning. Everything you do should be related to showing the business and showing the product. If you want to accelerate the success process then become an expert at the invitation so you have more people to show. Become an expert at promoting events so the people get the big picture sooner; otherwise, they tend to drift.

Once people join you in the business, they tend to take up part of your day. They'll be calling you and saying "Can you help me with some three way calls? Guess what I did today? Guess whom I'm showing? Can you help me show the business here or there?" And, the next thing you know, the day is gone and you didn't show anyone the product or the business for yourself. What's happened is you're not setting a good example. People will do what you do. The speed of the leader is the speed of the group.

Even if you are helping your people, you still have to continue to help yourself. Block out one or two hours of your day to work specifically on building **your** business. Then, give the rest of your day to your people, if you are full-time. If you're part-time, you need to take part of the time available for your own money producing activities as well. Show the business — show the product for yourself. Then leave the remainder of time to help your people show the business and the product. Remember that old duplication thing.

If you want your people to be out showing the business and showing the product, you have to be doing it too! If you ever stop showing the business for yourself and/or your people, you've hit the management mode. And when that happens it's easy to lose your day to managing your organization instead of building it. If you become a manager, so will your people. You will have an organization of managers.

You have to lead the way to success for your organization. Speaking of leading the way, that's exactly what we are going to be discussing in the next chapter: leadership. Believe me when I tell you, leaders aren't born—they are developed. And, the best way to lead is to first learn to follow. So, up to this point if you have learned anything, I hope you have learned to follow what your upline has taught you. If so, now you're ready to become a leader! If your upline is a master at developing leaders, they will have already put you in situations that test your abilities. With their help and guidance, you'll become a competent leader to your people.

CHAPTER 11
Can't Someone Else Lead?

Leading the way for your organization is up to you. It's part of the duplication process. In other words, you set the example by being a good follower and, in doing so you are teaching your people the first step in becoming a good leader. You teach them to be good followers. By being a good follower you have already started to lead.

Don't get overwhelmed with the responsibility of leadership. It is really something that can come quite easily. Through the process of building your business, learning the system and teaching the system to other people in your organization, you're leading whether you realize it or not. Most importantly, you're leading by example.

The Speed of the Leader Is the Speed of the Group

Whatever you want your people to do, and when you want them to do it, must be reinforced by you leading the way. Duplication! You work your business exactly the way you want your people to work their business. Duplication! You do it first. Duplication!

If you are new and want your people to progress quickly and attain higher levels of achievement quickly, move quickly. Learn the business right along with them. Check your ego at the door. You don't need to know it all first. Even though you are the sponsor, you will all be learning things side-by-side. This is not traditional business where you must learn before you do. In network marketing you learn and do at the same time.

The most important thing you are teaching them at this time is not just the systems and program, but how not to fear doing things that are bound to make them a bit uncomfortable. They'll see you are moving ahead and it will give them courage to push through their fears.

You will never learn everything there is to know before you sponsor others. Your job is to lead by example. You'll be building your business and learning right along with some of your downline. They'll understand that they, like you, can be building their business while they are learning, too.

Developing your business as quickly as you can that first 90 days is paramount. If you do it — they'll do it. Don't cheat them out of moving quickly because you're afraid you may not know how to answer all their questions or you may make a mistake here and there along the way. Your upline will be more than happy to help you and your distributors. It's great to have an upline to share the load.

Have the Courage to Be a Leader

Don't worry about having a perfect invitation the first time; just do it. Don't worry about having the perfect atmosphere or the perfect words for your first presentation; just do it. Don't worry about having perfect presentation materials; Just do it!

Jump right in there and be first. Be the first one in your upline and downline to hold a group meeting. Be the first one in your organization to take your business overseas. Be the first one in your group to register twenty top producers. Do it! Be first to set the example and the rest of your organization will follow.

Commit Yourself and So Will Your Organization

One of the biggest commitments you can make is to participate in all the events whether they are live events, conference calls or online presentations. Get your group excited about participating with you. Talk to them about investing time in their businesses in order to be the best they can be. When they participate, their downline will too. It's like a high-level production chain. The more participating, the more will get the bigger picture.

Participating in all the events, using the product/service, having product inventory, if applicable to your particular business, using the marketing tools available in your company, all of these will have a direct impact on what the rest of your downline does. Your people will follow your lead. One of the first questions someone you recruit will ask you is "How did you start your business?" In actuality, **your leadership role begins the day you sign**

your application. Everything you do will be followed by your people, so it's important that you do what you want them to duplicate.

It's Up to You To Set the Pace

One of the best things you can do when you give an opportunity presentation, whether it's in someone's home, a hotel, on a conference call or through an online presentation is that you have a guest of your own participating in the event. What you are doing is letting your downline know that you're leading by example. You're doing exactly what you expect them to do. You're setting the pace. Another good thing about having guests is that it never gives those in your organization the feeling that they are all you have. You don't want them thinking that if it weren't for them, you wouldn't have a business. Just keep showing the product and showing the business and you'll be an incredible inspiration.

Passing On the Leadership

I'll give you an example of how I pass on the leadership to my people when showing the business. I usually try to break the presentation down in my mind. I have an outline of what I want to say and when I want to say it. My presentation is easy to follow; it goes in these quick seven steps:

1. Introduce the speaker

2. Introduce trends and the industry

3. Introduce the company

4. Introduce the products

5. Describe the compensation program

6. Explain the rewards and awards that come from building the business, including company trips and bonuses

7. Training and support provided by our team

8. Testimonials from others

When I have a new person and I'm doing the first presentation for them, I will ask them to introduce me. If they can go into any part of the trend and the company, I want them to do that. The more of the presentation they can do, the quicker they will learn and the more confident they'll feel about going just a little further the next time. However, to reassure them, I tell them that the minute they feel they have gone far enough for their comfort, they can then pass the rest of the presentation on to me.

At the same time, they should be recording the entire presentation. They will then transcribe it and start to memorize the whole presentation. At our second presentation, they will present the trends and introduction of the company and then turn it over to me with an introduction. I will introduce the products, compensation program and the rewards and support. We just keep taking each presentation a step further into the process for them. That way they get to practice what they have already learned and feel confident with that part. Next they get to step into that uncomfortable zone and push themselves a little further. This process is done until the new person can take the presentation all the way to the end. If they begin to feel uncomfortable, they may turn it over to me at any given moment, and no one is the wiser. It's a proven process that works for everyone. At the same time, if that new person sponsors someone, they'll start to do the very beginning of the presentation.

There may be three people handling the presentation at any one time. The very new recruit will come forward and handle the introductions. Their sponsor might be presenting the industry and the company, then turn it over to the next upline to do the compensation program, the rewards, support and close.

See—Do—Teach

What we are doing is a concept in network marketing we call "see, do, teach." The person I sponsored saw me do it, they then do it, and now they can teach their new person how to do it. This is the process of transferring leadership. It's duplication! The same process works with the training. I require my new distributors to tape and learn the training as if they had to teach it. After they have taped a session, transcribed it, memorized the first part and practiced it, they then participate by doing that part in the actual training. Once they reach the part they are unfamiliar with, they pass it on to their sponsor. That way, you share the responsibility with your sponsor until it comes to the point that you can do it alone, with your sponsor in the audience observing your progress and cheering you on to a great presentation.

Three Ingredients to a Successful Business

There are three ingredients to a successful business: **communication, a business-building system** and **recognition**. These three things are critical to expanding your business. It's important that your distributors have constant communication so that they're up to date on events, new products and new ideas for showing the business and marketing the product.

They also need a step-by-step system for building their business so they know exactly what they should be doing. It is a track to run on.

The third ingredient, recognition, is perhaps one of the most important to sustain their momentum and excitement. Participating in events and being recognized for their accomplishments helps them to push ahead to the next goal. It's nice if you can have recognition events every 90 days. People can focus on short range goals for at least 90 days and reset their goals for the next 90 days. It's also important for their organization to see them edified. Let's take each one of these three ingredients separately and examine their importance.

Communication

Being in constant communication with your people will solidify your relationship and motivate them to greater heights. Through your constant communications you'll teach your downline to communicate with their people. You are duplicating proper communication skills. If they have a bad day, your encouraging communications remind them that it is still a viable business, and that you are just as committed today to helping them as you were in the good times. Communication lets them know that every network marketer has gone through similar circumstances and survived similar setbacks, yet they pressed forward to become top producers in the industry. That gives them the strength to continue.

Technology has made communication with distributors so much easier over the last decade. Conference calls and online presentations allow you to give trainings and opportunity presentations to large numbers of people around the world without ever leaving your office.

Reaching large numbers of people quickly has become simple. There are communication systems available that allow you to broadcast messages to your entire organization as often as you need. Email gives you the ability to distribute important information through your entire organization. It enables you to send the latest event schedule, information on products, latest updates and announcements

Voicemail or an answering machine is a must. You don't want to miss a message, plus you want to be able to use it as a screening mechanism when you're trying to get things done. It's sometimes difficult to get what you need to do for your own business completed while at the same time stay in touch with your organization and get back with them quickly. The outgoing message on your voicemail should be short and very professional. It should not be a message placed by a child. No dogs barking in the background. A sample message would be one such as: "No one is available to take your call at this time. If you will leave your name, number and a short message, if necessary, someone will return your call as soon as possible."

That message is brief, to the point, and it has one other important element. You haven't actually promised a return call. You've said that someone would return their call, if necessary. This prevents you from promising to return a call when you realize that it is not necessary to do so immediately. Don't simply say "Someone will return your call!" Tag on "… if necessary."

Be sure your service or machine allows you to change a message while you're on the road, and offers the convenience of checking your messages remotely.

If it is your goal to build a large networking business, answering the telephone can cut into a huge amount of your productive time. If a system of communication is followed, it should make it easier for you to keep setting that good example of showing the product and showing the business. At the same time, you'll be able to set aside planned time to return phone calls and assist your downline with their business and share in their victories. The most ideal situation is for you to communicate with your frontline, and they in turn communicate with their frontline, and so on and so on until everyone in the organization has received the necessary communications.

Occasionally you'll have a breakdown with someone who won't pass on the information, at which point you may want to consider eliminating them from the communication link. If I had someone in my frontline who didn't communicate to their frontline, I would get the e-mail addresses of their frontline, and I would bypass them by communicating directly with their frontline instead. It doesn't take long for that person to come to you asking for a second chance. There's nothing more embarrassing than when the organization knows things before their sponsor. That usually will solve your problem. I know because I have used it!

I had a frontline distributor who reached one of the highest positions in the company in spite of the fact that his communication with his frontline was almost nonexistent. Fortunately for him, his frontline distributors were very self-sufficient, plus I was a good communicator. When I realized e-mails were not getting forwarded, I merely by passed this frontline distributor and sent my communications to his frontline directly. It wasn't long before the embarrassment of knowing things after his group caused him to call me and beg for a second chance to pass on information.

Don't be afraid to take a hard stand once in a while. At times, the best of us needs someone to tell us the truth, even when it is something we may not want to hear. When you have something you have to tell someone that is a bit tough on them, remember to temper it with something that leaves them encouraged. If you are in their presence, it is a lot easier. For example, give them a gentle touch when you are delivering a harsher message. Let them know you care about them, that they have what it takes to be successful and you expected more from them. At the same time remind them of what they said they wanted to achieve, put your arm around them and let them know that you care for them. That is the reason you are having this little talk. It's more difficult over the phone. Encourage them and let them know you care and respect them then give them a solution to the problem. You can rebuild a strong communication chain, one little link at a time.

Teach to the Level of Your Distributor

In all communications, it's important that you spoon feed your people. Training is a form of communication, too. One of the biggest mistakes that I see distributors make is that they take everything they've learned over the last six months in network marketing and they try to cram it into the head of the new person who just started two days ago. It is not surprising that their new distributors are overwhelmed. It is not uncommon for them to become paralyzed and quit.

You wouldn't teach calculus to a third grader, would you? Of course you wouldn't! Your training should be set up accordingly. In other words, you should teach and communicate only that information necessary for that person in their present position to absorb properly and move to the next position. Once they've achieved that position, you can teach and communicate to them the information they're going to need to take them to the next position. After they've reached that level, teach and communicate the necessary information that will take them on up to the next level. Be selective in what you communicate, based on the level of that particular person. I sometimes refer to it as teaching to the grade level!

The Second Ingredient to Success—
Knowing the System

The most important word in network marketing, the word that should be tattooed to the inside of your eyelids, the word that should dominate every thing you say and do is: DUPLICATION. If you're trying anything new, the first question you should ask yourself is "Is it duplicatable?" If it isn't, for heaven's sake, don't do it!

Clone yourself. Encourage your distributors to become you. Practice the KISS system. It's a pass-it-down kind of business. The process breaks down if you haven't made every step of the way so simple that everyone can duplicate it. That's why you do it the same way every time so they can duplicate it. Pass on the information—pass on the system—pass on the process—pass on the leadership—pass on the REWARDS!

There will come a time when you will have an organization so large that you won't know everyone in your own organization. It will be inevitable that it will grow out of your reach. But, that's okay. If you knew everyone in your business, you would not be as successful.

This kind of growth is not manageable by traditional, conventional business practices. It is only manageable by being willing to follow a system, pass on that system, then let go and let it work.

Being duplicatable is not always an easy task, especially when you are dealing with people and each one is different and circumstances change. You will need to constantly monitor everything you do and say. Time after time, I've seen people who will let their ego get in the way. They get more concerned with the accolades, the pats on the back and spouting a new idea or untried concept. It's usually an idea or concept they haven't proven, yet they are willing to share it with other people, some of whom may not be in their group. Don't fall into the position of having to prove or disprove somebody else's theory. If they're going to preach it, let them teach it — only after they have proven it works with their own business first. Anything that is shared with someone else's group should be a proven method of successful practice, and should be cleared with the group leadership first. To do it any differently would be reckless and disrespectful.

The bottom line is not how many pats on the back you get. Real success comes by teaching something that people can learn and follow. These are fundamental methods that don't change from week to week. The program is a step-by-step system: a step-by-step system of getting started, a step-by-step system of recruiting, a step-by-step system of building an organization and a step-by-step system for building leaders.

The Third Ingredient for Success—Promoting Events

Promotion is one of the least understood yet one of the highest paying skills you can learn. Promoting events properly is the second greatest talent you need to acquire; the first is inviting people to see the business. Promotion is essential and will accelerate your success. We talked about this earlier, but repetition and duplication is the key to learning, so it's worth saying one more time. Having a vision of the business, **the big picture**, is really what it takes to motivate yourself and others to create tremendous businesses. Put action behind your commitment. Without the bigger picture, people just go through the motions of being involved in the business without really being on fire!

It would be nice if people caught the big picture the first time they saw the business, but unfortunately, that's not the case. There are people who will sometimes need to be in a business, around the events, around the people for six months or longer before they ever really get the bigger picture. Suddenly a light goes off in their heads. That's my "light bulb theory." It's the old "I've got it" concept. I make light of this (no pun intended), but I sometimes think if everyone would be plugged in at a meeting, I would see light bulbs going off periodically during the event every time they finally got the big picture. It may have been said a hundred times, but they just weren't plugged in before that particular meeting. Now, what would have happened had they not attended? No light, no productivity, pretty soon — no business! Promotion is the key to getting them to attend these events.

Sometimes the message just doesn't come across in the beginning. It may be a testimonial that turns on their light bulb. It might be a conversation with someone in the same occupation that they meet at an event that gets them turned on. Sometimes a guest speaker will happen to say that one thing that reaches your guest.

I had a very talented basketball coach in my business. He had credibility, charisma and contacts, but I couldn't seem to get him going in this business. After a great deal of coercing, I finally got him to attend a meeting. At the end of this meeting one of the testimonials was a former student and basketball player he had coached. This former student shared with everyone how much money he was making every week selling the company's product. As it turned out, it was more than the coach was making. Boy was he angry! But a light bulb went off that night for that coach and he got the bigger picture. He was on fire and hit the top position in record time.

You never know exactly what it is that's going to set off the light, but don't deprive them of the opportunity.

Invite your people to participate in every single event. It is up to you to promote the event like there's no tomorrow. Talk about it like it was the best opportunity to come along since Coca Cola. Tell them it could advance their business ten-fold by participating in the event.

Create an urgency to participate in the events. Create a fear of loss so that your distributors will make the effort. You'll be amazed at how dramatically this can advance someone's business. Getting the bigger picture is everything, and that is exactly what participating in live events, conference calls and online presentations can do for those in your organization. Remember what I said earlier — **until the vision is in their head, it's not going to come out of their mouth properly;** the bigger their vision, the bigger their story. Your distributors can only relate and talk about whatever it is they truly believe and understand. If you're not reaching them, someone during the event will. Give them that chance.

Be Fun to Be Around

Although you should be taking your business seriously, don't always take yourself so seriously. Have fun. Relax! It'll be more fun for you and for your organization when you can laugh at yourself and get others laughing. Develop your relationships and take them to a different level.

If you are in the middle of an important presentation and you make a mistake, laugh at yourself. It gives your audience an opportunity to relate to you. It's human to make mistakes. There is power in laughter. I have felt more freedom and had more fun in network marketing than in any other business with which I have been involved. If I want everything I do to be duplicatable, my organization will be laughing and having fun right along with me. We only go around once, so have fun and develop the biggest, deepest circle of friends you can.

CHAPTER 12

Whew! You Made It!

I am so proud of you. You made it to the last chapter. Now you have all of the knowledge necessary to build a fantastic business and it is all at your fingertips. Remember to use this book as a constant resource. I hope you highlighted things, made notes and really marked it up because that tells me it has brought value and will continue to bring great wisdom and support to you.

Now, comes the hard part: overcoming you, getting yourself out of the way of your own success, overcoming whatever it is that is holding you back. Like the homeless man said as the rich man in the Bentley drove by, "That could be me, if not for I." Belief in yourself and your abilities can be hard for some but it is definitely obtainable. After all, if success is for the taking, why not you?

It's not uncommon for new distributors to enter the network marketing arena in a fragile state. Sometimes they enter out of necessity rather than from their strength of conviction to own their own business. For this reason personal attention and support to help them develop their confidence and rebuild their self-esteem is so important. It's hard to sell others on the belief that they can accomplish something when you don't believe it yourself. That's why I want to spend a few moments on "you."

A recruiting advertisement for the United States Military encourages you to, "Be all you can be." It is a commercial to sell you on you. Success is out there for the taking, so why not you? After all, you deserve it. And so do the people you care about.

You are here for a reason. Your life has meaning and a mission. You have a special purpose. There is a reason you are alive and here today. You are a miracle, a survivor of survivors. How many times could your genetic link have been broken? Could it have been on a slave ship from Africa or a refugee boat from Cuba? Could it have been a serious illness or accident? Could it have been broken during the plague, in the Civil War or maybe even the Vietnam War? What were the chances at conception that the right combination would be you? The fact that you are here today is a miracle all in itself.

You are so amazing. From the day you were born you were equipped with the ability to live 200 years. You are so amazing that if the energy in your brain when working could be harnessed and converted into electrical power, you could provide enough electrical power for Los Angeles 24 hours a day for two years. Your brain could compete with some of the best computers. You have the ability to read 2,000 to 4,000 words per minute. You are so incredible.

All you need to do is to start believing in you and tap into the genius within. I know it sounds simpler than it is, but you can accomplish all of this and become all-powerful, one step at a time. With each step in building your self-esteem you will grow in confidence. And I am here to help you through the baby steps until you are in a full sprint.

Remember, what holds people back is not what they think they are, but what they think they are not.

There are four things I did to help build my self-esteem

1. Read personal development books.

2. Listened to uplifting personal development programs.

3. Wrote personal affirmations that I read many times every day.

4. Practiced self-talk to lift myself up and overcome my fears (your subconscious loves your own voice).

We all have our own battles to fight and obstacles to overcome. Network marketing is such a great vehicle for personal discovery and development. Understand that we all have different circumstances. Each of us has different backgrounds, experiences and desires. To me, that's the beauty of network marketing. It doesn't matter. Unlike the traditional corporate business world, network marketing doesn't discriminate based on your gender, race, nationality, income level, education, past experience, etc. You are the only one who says whether you will make it or not. You decide whether to follow the steps of success or let a few rejections stop you in your tracks.

Remember, successful network marketing is like following a recipe wherein the first step is to internally make the decision that you want to succeed. That is your first goal. Nothing you do before you truly internalize that resolve will make much of a difference. Once you decide to start, commit for one year to all-out effort with no turning back.

The next step to the recipe is discipline. Day in and day out you need to do what it takes to build a strong organization. Discipline is simply a matter of making yourself do what you said you would do long after the feeling you had when you said it has passed. Regardless of the weather, even if you feel sick, and especially if you are getting bored with the routine, discipline yourself to pick up the phone or get out your front door. This is what separates the successful from the unsuccessful. I have often heard that it is what we do when no one is around that is the true test of one's character. Much of the work you will do in network marketing will be done when no one is watching. At such times, the journey of success may be lonely, but that's why we give such accolades to those who reach the top. We know the price they paid. All I can say is stick with it, keeping the end in mind and you will reap the rewards.

The third step is to not take rejection personally. I will never forget how liberated I felt when I finally realized that when people told me "no" they were not personally rejecting me. You need to make your own breakthrough in this area and understand it's a numbers game. Success is in the number of times you show the product and opportunity. Keep in mind that it doesn't matter what the product is as long as you believe in it, so you can speak with conviction. Even if you attach it to the back of your car and drive around town, someone will eventually ask you about it. You just need to tell your story the best you know how. The numbers game is a fact. With every "yes" there will be a "no." Don't let discouragement creep in.

The fourth step is duplication. Don't think you have to come up with your own original system for becoming a successful network marketer. The system is already in place. The more you follow a well-designed plan, proven through past use, the more those with you will see how it is done and mimic your actions. In turn, they will also be successful, which will fortify and strengthen your own organization and lead to a self-sustaining business with true residual income.

Perhaps the most important item in the recipe for success is to have fun. Granted, not every day will find you completely excited about life and enjoying yourself one hundred percent; after all, you're still human. But overall, network marketing is the most enjoyable business I've ever been a part of in my life. It has also been the most life altering. I have more dear friends because of network marketing than I would have ever imagined. I have seen parts of the world I never thought I would see. And I have discovered more about myself and developed personally far beyond my wildest dreams because of the platform network marketing creates for personal development.

I want to take a moment to congratulate you for finishing this book. It tells me you are serious about this journey called network marketing. But it also says you're open-minded, teachable, willing to learn, practice and develop a "whatever it takes" attitude. Don't ever lose that. It's refreshing, especially when a leader remains teachable, knowing that some of their greatest lessons could come through the eyes of a fresh, new, bright distributor.

Let me share with you some secrets: pass on the leadership and the glory, embrace your people's goals as your own, know when to let go, let your leaders shine and teach your people to be more successful than you. Those are the greatest secrets for true success in network marketing. And they are your ticket to truly owning yourself.

Have a wonderful journey.

About the Author

While pursuing her doctorate degree at Kent State University, networking icon Paula Pritchard became disillusioned by the inability to advance financially in the collegiate world. With a bachelor's and master's degree already under her belt, she was working on her Ph.D. when she decided to attend her first network marketing meeting. She was considering the idea of making some extra cash that summer. That decision lead her to become a multi- million dollar earner. Paula shares in this book her networking philosophy that propelled her to the top level of six different network marketing companies.

Her first network marketing experience was in Amway. Out of over one million distributors at the time, Paula was the first single woman in the United States to reach the distinguished position of Diamond. Since Amway, Paula has achieved major successes with other networking companies including: Herbalife, NSA, Quorum and MXI. She spearheaded the expansion of four companies into Europe. In addition, she built a business from the ground up with over 200,000 people spread over 15 countries. As one of the top and most consistent performers in the network marketing industry, she has proven time and time again that her methods work. Her techniques of building a large successful business have been widely tested and used over and over again. It is truly rare to find an individual who has made it to the top of six different companies in separate markets appealing to diverse demographics.

In this book Paula takes her readers through clear and logical steps that remove the mystery surrounding how she became successful in network marketing. In addition she teaches her readers how to identify and achieve their networking dreams, and she lends support, encouragement, insight and comprehension to those experiencing the ups and downs of network marketing. No matter at what stage your business is, this book will give you the know how to recruit, train and lead in network marketing

Lightning Source UK Ltd.
Milton Keynes UK
UKOW052308030113

204386UK00001B/7/P